Stories o

Rossiter Johnson

Alpha Editions

This edition published in 2024

ISBN : 9789362929327

Design and Setting By
Alpha Editions
www.alphaedis.com
Email - info@alphaedis.com

Contents

LITTLE CLASSICS.

It is not more difficult for the mineralogist to define a metal, than for the critic to define a classic. No attribute or property of metal can be mentioned,—hardness, brittleness, malleability, magnetism, lustre,—but some acknowledged metal can be found which lacks it. So when we come to define what is classic in literature, we find not a single quality that may not be dispensed with, or that is not lacking in some universally accepted and canonized piece of composition. Is age a requisite? Consider Mr. Lincoln's speech at Gettysburg, which was recognized as classic and immortal the hour it was flashed from the wires and printed or misprinted in the five thousand journals of the land. Is perfection of plot or unity of design necessary? "David Copperfield" can hardly be said to have a plot, and the "Merchant of Venice" is notably lacking in unity. Is detailed grammatical and idiomatic correctness indispensable? Then how few are the absolute masters of English prose! It is with some feeling of embarrassment at this lack of any perfect test, that I have gathered the contents of these volumes and ventured to call them Little Classics. And yet the genuine lovers of literature, setting aside all attempt at conscious definition, and following only their artistic instincts, will not seriously differ in their opinion as to what deserves the name of classic and bears the warrant of immortality.

The performance of this task has suggested the idea that, in romantic fiction, ours is the day of small things,—small as the diamond and the violet are small. Going freely through English literature to gather little classics, I have been surprised at finding so few that antedate the present century. Hawthorne, De Quincey, Poe, and Dr. Brown have put within the compass of a few pages as much plot and character, as much pathos, humor, human nature, metaphysical speculation, and dramatic effect, as commonly suffice for a full-length romance. The ponderous novel cannot be said to have had its day; but the indications are that it must soon cease to have more than its day. The work of art which, embodying a sacred principle or a living idea, condenses its plot, its moral, and its effective climax into the limits of a single sitting must, in an age of crowding books and rushing readers, possess a decisive advantage over the unwieldy conventional novel, with its caravan of characters and its long bewilderment of detail. The Ark of the Deluge may crumble on the mountain, but the Ark of the Covenant is borne by the people through all their wanderings, and enshrined in the temple when they rest.

If the prevailing cast of these tales is sombre and tragic, it is not from any design on the part of the compiler; it is because, being true to nature and to human experience, they follow the inevitable course of human destiny. In the broad light of our daily life lie the superficial, the ephemeral, and the inessential; in its shadow lie God's solemn mysteries and man's profoundest studies. That in us which humor appeals to is selfish, and finds its limit within the narrow boundary of one's own being. That which pathos awakens is sacrificial in its tendency, and stretches a protecting arm, or offers a sympathetic heart, to all the world.

NEW YORK, February, 1874.

ETHAN BRAND.

BY NATHANIEL HAWTHORNE.

Bartram the lime-burner, a rough, heavy-looking man, begrimed with charcoal, sat watching his kiln, at nightfall, while his little son played at building houses with the scattered fragments of marble, when, on the hillside below them, they heard a roar of laughter, not mirthful, but slow, and even solemn, like a wind shaking the boughs of the forest.

"Father, what is that?" asked the little boy, leaving his play, and pressing betwixt his father's knees.

"O, some drunken man, I suppose!" answered the lime-burner; "some merry fellow from the bar-room in the village, who dared not laugh loud enough within doors, lest he should blow the roof of the house off. So here he is, shaking his jolly sides at the foot of Graylock."

"But, father," said the child, more sensitive than the obtuse, middle-aged clown, "he does not laugh like a man that is glad. So the noise frightens me!"

"Don't be a fool, child!" cried his father, gruffly. "You will never make a man, I do believe; there istoo much of your mother in you. I have known the rustling of a leaf startle you. Hark! Here comes the merry fellow, now. You shall see that there is no harm in him."

Bartram and his little son, while they were talking thus, sat watching the same lime-kiln that had been the scene of Ethan Brand's solitary and meditative life, before he began his search for the Unpardonable Sin. Many years had elapsed since the portentous night when the IDEA was first developed. The kiln, however, on the mountain-side, stood unimpaired, and was in nothing changed since he had thrown his dark thoughts into the intense glow of its furnace, and melted them, as it were, into the one thought that took possession of his life. It was a rude, round, tower-like structure, about twenty feet high, heavily built of rough stones, and with a hillock of earth heaped about the larger part of its circumference; so that the blocks and fragments of marble might be drawn by cart-loads, and thrown in at the top. There was an opening at the bottom of the tower like an oven-mouth, but large enough to admit a man in a stooping posture, and provided with a massive iron door. With the smoke and jets of flame issuing from the chinks and crevices of this door, which seemed to give admittance into the hillside, it resembled nothing so much as the private entrance to the infernal regions, which the shepherds of the Delectable Mountains were accustomed to show to pilgrims.

There are many such lime-kilns in that tract of country, for the purpose of burning the white marble which composes a large part of the substance of the hills. Some of them, built years ago and long deserted, with weeds growing in the vacant round of the interior, which is open to the sky, and grass and wild-flowers rooting themselves into the chinks of the stones, look already like relics of antiquity, and may yet be overspread with the lichens of centuries to come. Others, where the lime-burner still feeds his daily and night-long fire, afford points of interest to the wanderer among the hills who seats himself on a log of wood or a fragment of marble, to hold a chat with the solitary man. It is a lonesome, and, when the character is inclined to thought, may be an intensely thoughtful occupation; as it proved in the case of Ethan Brand, who had mused to such strange purpose, in days gone by, while the fire in this very kiln was burning.

The man who now watched the fire was of a different order, and troubled himself with no thoughts save the very few that were requisite to his business. At frequent intervals he flung back the clashing weight of the iron door, and, turning his face from the insufferable glare, thrust in huge logs of oak, or stirred the immense brands with a long pole. Within the furnace were seen the curling and riotous flames, and the burning marble, almost molten with the intensity of heat; while without the reflection of the fire quivered on the dark intricacy of the surrounding forest, and showed in the foreground a bright and ruddy little picture of the hut, the spring beside its door, the athletic and coal-begrimed figure of the lime-burner, and the half-frightened child, shrinking into the protection of his father's shadow. And when again the iron door was closed, then reappeared the tenderlight of the half-full moon, which vainly strove to trace out the indistinct shapes of the neighboring mountains; and, in the upper sky, there was a flitting congregation of clouds, still faintly tinged with the rosy sunset, though thus far down into the valley the sunshine had vanished long and long ago.

The little boy now crept still closer to his father, as footsteps were heard ascending the hillside, and a human form thrust aside the bushes that clustered beneath the trees.

"Halloo! who is it?" cried the lime-burner, vexed at his son's timidity, yet half infected by it. "Come forward, and show yourself, like a man, or I'll fling this chunk of marble at your head!"

"You offer me a rough welcome," said a gloomy voice, as the unknown man drew nigh. "Yet I neither claim nor desire a kinder one, even at my own fireside."

To obtain a distincter view, Bartram threw open the iron door of the kiln, whence immediately issued a gush of fierce light that smote full upon the stranger's face and figure. To a careless eye there appeared nothing very remarkable in his aspect, which was that of a man in a coarse, brown, country-made suit of clothes, tall and thin, with the staff and heavy shoes of a wayfarer. As he advanced, he fixed his eyes—which were very bright—intently upon the brightness of the furnace, as if he beheld, or expected to behold, some object worthy of note within it.

"Good evening, stranger," said the lime-burner; "whence come you, so late in the day?"

"I come from my search," answered the wayfarer; "for, at last, it is finished."

"Drunk!—or crazy!" muttered Bartram to himself. "I shall have trouble with the fellow. The sooner I drive him away the better."

The little boy, all in a tremble, whispered to his father, and begged him to shut the door of the kiln, so that there might not be so much light; for that there was something in the man's face which he was afraid to look at, yet could not look away from. And, indeed, even the lime-burner's dull and torpid sense began to be impressed by an indescribable something in that thin, rugged, thoughtful visage, with the grizzled hair hanging wildly about it, and those deeply sunken eyes, which gleamed like fires within the entrance of a mysterious cavern. But, as he closed the door, the stranger turned towards him, and spoke in a quiet, familiar way, that made Bartram feel as if he were a sane and sensible man, after all.

"Your task draws to an end, I see," said he. "This marble has already been burning three days. A few hours more will convert the stone to lime."

"Why, who are you?" exclaimed the lime-burner. "You seem as well acquainted with my business as I am myself."

"And well I may be," said the stranger; "for I followed the same craft many a long year, and here, too, on this very spot. But you are a new-comer in these parts. Did you never hear of Ethan Brand?"

"The man that went in search of the Unpardonable Sin?" asked Bartram, with a laugh.

"The same," answered the stranger. "He has found what he sought, and therefore he comes back again."

"What! then you are Ethan Brand himself?" cried the lime-burner, in amazement. "I am a new-comer here, as you say, and they call it eighteen years since you left the foot of Graylock. But I can tell you, the good folks still talk about Ethan Brand, in the village yonder, and what a strange errand took him away from his lime-kiln. Well, and so you have found the Unpardonable Sin?"

"Even so!" said the stranger, calmly.

"If the question is a fair one," proceeded Bartram, "where might it be?"

Ethan Brand laid his finger on his own heart.

"Here!" replied he.

And then, without mirth in his countenance, but as if moved by an involuntary recognition of the infinite absurdity of seeking throughout the world for what was the closest of all things to himself, and looking into every heart, save his own, for what was hidden in no other breast, he broke into a laugh of scorn. It was the same slow, heavy laugh, that had almost appalled the lime-burner when it heralded the wayfarer's approach.

The solitary mountain-side was made dismal by it. Laughter, when out of place, mistimed, or bursting forth from a disordered state of feeling, may be the most terrible modulation of the human voice. The laughter of one asleep, even if it be a little child,—the madman's laugh,—the wild, screaming laugh of a born idiot,—are sounds that we sometimes tremble to hear, and would always willingly forget. Poets have imagined no utterance of fiends or hobgoblins so fearfully appropriate as a laugh. And even the obtuse lime-burner felt his nerves shaken, as this strange man looked inward at his ownheart, and burst into laughter that rolled away into the night, and was indistinctly reverberated among the hills.

"Joe," said he to his little son, "scamper down to the tavern in the village, and tell the jolly fellows there that Ethan Brand has come back, and that he has found the Unpardonable Sin!"

The boy darted away on his errand, to which Ethan Brand made no objection, nor seemed hardly to notice it. He sat on a log of wood, looking steadfastly at the iron door of the kiln. When the child was out of sight, and his swift and light footsteps ceased to be heard treading first on the fallen leaves and then on the rocky mountain-path, the lime-burner began to regret his departure. He felt that the little fellow's presence had been a barrier between his guest and himself, and that he must now deal, heart to heart, with a man who, on his own confession, had committed the one only crime for which Heaven could afford no mercy. That crime, in its indistinct blackness, seemed to overshadow him. The lime-burner's own sins rose up within him, and made his memory riotous with a throng of evil shapes that asserted their kindred with the Master Sin, whatever it might be, which it was within the scope of man's corrupted nature to conceive and cherish.

They were all of one family; they went to and fro between his breast and Ethan Brand's, and carried dark greetings from one to the other.

Then Bartram remembered the stories which had grown traditionary in reference to this strange man, who had come upon him like a shadow of the night, and was making himself at home in his old place, afterso long absence that the dead people, dead and buried for years, would have had more right to be at home, in any familiar spot, than he. Ethan Brand, it was said, had conversed with Satan himself in the lurid blaze of this very kiln. The legend had been matter of mirth heretofore, but looked grisly now. According to this tale, before Ethan Brand departed on his search, he had been accustomed to evoke a fiend from the hot furnace of the lime-kiln, night after night, in order to confer with him about the Unpardonable Sin; the man and the fiend each laboring to frame the image of some mode of guilt which could neither be atoned for nor forgiven. And, with the first gleam of light upon the mountain-top, the fiend crept in at the iron door, there to abide the intensest element of fire, until again summoned forth to share in the dreadful task of extending man's possible guilt beyond the scope of Heaven's else infinite mercy.

While the lime-burner was struggling with the horror of these thoughts, Ethan Brand rose from the log, and flung open the door of the kiln. The action was in such accordance with the idea in Bartram's mind, that he almost expected to see the Evil One issue forth, red-hot from the raging furnace.

"Hold! hold!" cried he, with a tremulous attempt to laugh; for he was ashamed of his fears, although they overmastered him. "Don't, for mercy's sake, bring out your devil now!"

"Man!" sternly replied Ethan Brand, "what need have I of the devil? I have left him behind me, on my track. It is with such half-way sinners as you that he busies himself. Fear not, because I open the door. Ido but act by old custom, and am going to trim your fire, like a lime-burner, as I was once."

He stirred the vast coals, thrust in more wood, and bent forward to gaze into the hollow prison-house of the fire, regardless of the fierce glow that reddened upon his face. The lime-burner sat watching him, and half suspected his strange guest of a purpose, if not to evoke a fiend, at least to plunge bodily into the flames, and thus vanish from the sight of man. Ethan Brand, however, drew quietly back, and closed the door of the kiln.

"I have looked," said he, "into many a human heart that was seven times hotter with sinful passions than yonder furnace is with fire. But I found not there what I sought. No, not the Unpardonable Sin!"

"What is the Unpardonable Sin?" asked the lime-burner; and then he shrank farther from his companion, trembling lest his question should be answered.

"It is a sin that grew within my own breast," replied Ethan Brand, standing erect, with a pride that distinguishes all enthusiasts of his stamp. "A sin that grew nowhere else! The sin of an intellect that triumphed over the sense of brotherhood with man and reverence for God, and sacrificed everything to its own mighty claims! The only sin that deserves a recompense of immortal agony! Freely, were it to do again, would I incur the guilt. Unshrinkingly I accept the retribution!"

"The man's head is turned," muttered the lime-burner to himself. "He may be a sinner, like the rest of us,—nothing more, likely,—but, I'll be sworn, he is a madman too."

Nevertheless he felt uncomfortable at his situation, alone with Ethan Brand on the wild mountain-side, and was right glad to hear the rough murmur of tongues, and the footsteps of what seemed a pretty numerous party, stumbling over the stones and rustling through the underbrush. Soon appeared the whole lazy regiment that was wont to infest the village tavern, comprehending three or four individuals who had drunk flip beside the bar-room fire through all the winters, and smoked their pipes beneath the stoop through all the summers, since Ethan Brand's departure. Laughing boisterously, and mingling all their voices together in unceremonious talk, they now burst into the moonshine and narrow streaks of firelight that illuminated the open space before the lime-kiln. Bartram set the door ajar again, flooding the spot with light, that the whole company might get a fair view of Ethan Brand, and he of them.

There, among other old acquaintances, was a once ubiquitous man, now almost extinct, but whom we were formerly sure to encounter at the hotel of every thriving village throughout the country. It was the stage-agent. The present specimen of the genus was a wilted and smoke-dried man, wrinkled and red-nosed, in a smartly cut, brown, bobtailed coat, with brass buttons, who, for a length of time unknown, had kept his desk and corner in the bar-room, and was still puffing what seemed to be the same cigar that he had lighted twenty years before. He had great fame as a dry joker, though, perhaps, less on account of any intrinsic humor than from a certain flavor of brandy-toddy and tobacco-smoke, which impregnatedall his ideas and expressions, as well as his person. Another well-remembered though strangely altered face was that of Lawyer Giles, as people still called him in courtesy; an elderly ragamuffin, in his soiled shirt-sleeves and tow-cloth trousers. This poor fellow had been an attorney, in what he called his better days, a sharp practitioner, and in great vogue among the village litigants; but flip and sling and toddy and cocktails, imbibed at all hours, morning, noon, and night, had caused him to slide from intellectual to various kinds and degrees of bodily labor, till at last, to adopt his own phrase, he slid into a soap-vat. In other words, Giles was now a soap-boiler, in a small way. He had come to be but the fragment of a human being, a part of one foot having been chopped off by an axe, and an entire hand torn away by the devilish grip of a steam-engine. Yet, though the corporeal hand was gone, a spiritual member remained; for, stretching forth the stump, Giles steadfastly averred that he felt an invisible thumb and fingers with as vivid a sensation as before the real ones were amputated. A maimed and miserable wretch he was; but one, nevertheless, whom the world could not trample on, and had no right to scorn, either in this or any previous stage of his misfortunes, since he had still kept up the courage and spirit of a man, asked nothing in charity, and with his one hand—and that the left one—fought a stern battle against want and hostile circumstances.

Among the throng, too, came another personage, who, with certain points of similarity to Lawyer Giles, had many more of difference. It was the village doctor, aman of some fifty years, a purple-visaged, rude, and brutal, yet half-gentlemanly figure, with something wild, ruined, and desperate in his talk, and in all the details of his gesture and manners. Brandy possessed this man like an evil spirit, and made him as surly and savage as a wild beast, and as miserable as a lost soul; but there was supposed to be in him such wonderful skill, such native gifts of healing, beyond any which medical science could impart, that society caught hold of him, and would not let him sink out of its reach. So, swaying to and fro upon his horse, and grumbling thick accents at the bed-side, he visited all the sick-chambers for miles about among the mountain towns, and sometimes raised a dying man, as it were, by miracle, or quite as often, no doubt, sent his patient to a grave that was dug many a year too soon. The doctor had an everlasting pipe in his mouth, and, as somebody said, in allusion to his habit of swearing, it was always alight with hell-fire.

These three worthies pressed forward, and greeted Ethan Brand each after his own fashion, earnestly inviting him to partake of the contents of a certain black bottle, in which, as they averred, he would find something far better worth seeking for than the Unpardonable Sin. No mind, which has wrought itself by intense and solitary meditation into a high state of enthusiasm, can endure the kind of contact with low and vulgar modes of thought and feeling to which Ethan Brand was now subjected. It made him doubt,—and, strange to say, it was a painful doubt,—whether he had indeed found the Unpardonable Sin, and found it within himself. The whole question on which he had exhausted life, and more than life, looked like a delusion.

"Leave me," he said bitterly, "ye brute beasts, that have made yourselves so, shrivelling up your souls with fiery liquors! I have done with you. Years and years ago I groped into your hearts, and found nothing there for my purpose. Get ye gone!"

"Why, you uncivil scoundrel," cried the fierce doctor, "is that the way you respond to the kindness of your best friends? Then let me tell you the truth. You have no more found the Unpardonable Sin than yonder boy Joe has. You are but a crazy fellow,—I told you so twenty years ago,—neither better nor worse than a crazy fellow, and the fit companion of old Humphrey, here!"

He pointed to an old man, shabbily dressed, with long white hair, thin visage, and unsteady eyes. For some years past this aged person had been wandering about among the hills, inquiring of all travellers whom he met for his daughter. The girl, it seemed, had gone off with a company of circus-performers; and occasionally tidings of her came to the village, and fine stories were told of her glittering appearance as she rode on horseback in the ring, or performed marvellous feats on the tight-rope.

The white-haired father now approached Ethan Brand, and gazed unsteadily into his face.

"They tell me you have been all over the earth," said he, wringing his hands with earnestness. "You must have seen my daughter, for she makes a grand figure in the world, and everybody goes to see her. Did she send any word to her old father, or say when she was coming back?"

Ethan Brand's eye quailed beneath the old man's. That daughter, with a cold and remorseless purpose, Ethan Brand had made the subject of a psychological experiment, and wasted, absorbed, and perhaps annihilated her soul, in the process.

"Yes," murmured he, turning away from the hoary wanderer; "it is no delusion. There is an Unpardonable Sin!"

While these things were passing, a merry scene was going forward in the area of cheerful light, beside the spring and before the door of the hut. A number of the youth of the village, young men and girls, had hurried up the hillside, impelled by curiosity to see Ethan Brand, the hero of so many a legend familiar to their childhood. Finding nothing, however, very remarkable in his aspect, nothing but a sunburnt wayfarer, in plain garb and dusty shoes, who sat looking into the fire, as if he fancied pictures among the coals,—these young people speedily grew tired of observing him. As it happened, there was other amusement at hand. An old German Jew, travelling with a diorama on his back, was passing down the mountain-road toward the village just as the party turned aside from it, and, in hopes of eking out the profits of the day, the showman had kept them company to the lime-kiln.

"Come, old Dutchman," cried one of the young men, "let us see your pictures, if you can swear they are worth looking at!"

"O yes, Captain," answered the Jew,—whether as a matter of courtesy or craft, he styled everybody Captain,—"I shall show you, indeed, some very superb pictures!"

So, placing his box in a proper position, he invited the young men and girls to look through the glass orifices of the machine, and proceeded to exhibit a series of the most outrageous scratchings and daubings, as specimens of the fine arts, that ever an itinerant showman had the face to impose upon his circle of spectators. The pictures were worn out, moreover, tattered, full of cracks and wrinkles, dingy with tobacco-smoke, and otherwise in a most pitiable condition. Some purported to be cities, public edifices, and ruined castles in Europe; others represented Napoleon's battles and Nelson's sea-fights; and in the midst of these would be seen a gigantic, brown, hairy hand,—which might have been mistaken for the Hand of Destiny, though, in truth, it was only the showman's,—pointing its forefinger to various scenes of the conflict, whilst its owner gave historical illustrations. When, with much merriment at its abominable deficiency of merit, the exhibition was concluded, the German bade little Joe put his head into the box. Viewed through the magnifying-glasses, the boy's round, rosy visage assumed the strangest imaginable aspect of an immense Titanic child, the mouth grinning broadly, and the eyes and every other feature overflowing with fun at the joke. Suddenly, however, that merry face turned pale, and its expression changed to horror, for this easily impressed and excitable child had become sensible that the eye of Ethan Brand was fixed upon him through the glass.

"You make the little man to be afraid, Captain," said the German Jew, turning up the dark and strong outline of his visage, from his stooping posture. "But lookagain, and, by chance, I shall cause you to see somewhat that is very fine, upon my word!"

Ethan Brand gazed into the box for an instant, and then starting back, looked fixedly at the German. What had he seen? Nothing, apparently; for a curious youth, who had peeped in almost at the same moment, beheld only a vacant space of canvas.

"I remember you now," muttered Ethan Brand to the showman.

"Ah, Captain," whispered the Jew of Nuremberg, with a dark smile, "I find it to be a heavy matter in my show-box,—this Unpardonable Sin! By my faith, Captain, it has wearied my shoulders, this long day, to carry it over the mountain."

"Peace," answered Ethan Brand, sternly, "or get thee into the furnace yonder!"

The Jew's exhibition had scarcely concluded, when a great, elderly dog—that seemed to be his own master, as no person in the company laid claim to him—saw fit to render himself the object of public notice. Hitherto, he had shown himself a very quiet, well-disposed old dog, going round from one to another, and, by way of being sociable, offering his rough head to be patted by any kindly hand that would take so much trouble. But now, all of a sudden, this grave and venerable quadruped, of his own mere motion, and without the slightest suggestion from anybody else, began to run round after his tail, which, to heighten the absurdity of the proceeding, was a great deal shorter than it should have been. Never was seen such headlong eagerness in pursuit of an object that could not possibly be attained; never washeard such a tremendous outbreak of growling, snarling, barking, and snapping,—as if one end of the ridiculous brute's body were at deadly and most unforgivable enmity with the other. Faster and faster, round about went the cur; and faster and still faster fled the unapproachable brevity of his tail; and louder and fiercer grew his yells of rage and animosity; until, utterly exhausted, and as far from the goal as ever, the foolish old dog ceased his performance as suddenly as he had begun it. The next moment he was as mild, quiet, sensible, and respectable in his deportment, as when he first scraped acquaintance with the company.

As may be supposed, the exhibition was greeted with universal laughter, clapping of hands, and shouts of encore, to which the canine performer responded by wagging all that there was to wag of his tail, but appeared totally unable to repeat his very successful effort to amuse the spectators.

Meanwhile Ethan Brand had resumed his seat upon the log, and moved, it might be, by a perception of some remote analogy between his own case and that of this self-pursuing cur, he broke into the awful laugh, which, more than any other token, expressed the condition of his inward being. From that moment the merriment of the party was at an end; they stood aghast, dreading lest the inauspicious sound should be reverberated around the horizon, and that mountain would thunder it to mountain, and so the horror be prolonged upon their ears. Then, whispering one to another that it was late,—that the moon was almost down,—that the August night was growing chill,—they hurried homewards,leaving the lime-burner and little Joe to deal as they might with their unwelcome guest. Save for these three human beings, the open space on the hillside was a solitude, set in a vast gloom of forest. Beyond that darksome verge the firelight glimmered on the stately trunks and almost black foliage of pines, intermixed with the lighter verdure of sapling oaks, maples, and poplars, while here and there lay the gigantic corpses of dead trees, decaying on the leaf-strewn soil. And it seemed to little Joe—a timorous and imaginative child—that the silent forest was holding its breath, until some fearful thing should happen.

Ethan Brand thrust more wood into the fire, and closed the door of the kiln; then looking over his shoulder at the lime-burner and his son, he bade, rather than advised, them to retire to rest.

"For myself, I cannot sleep," said he. "I have matters that it concerns me to meditate upon. I will watch the fire, as I used to do in the old time."

"And call the devil out of the furnace to keep you company, I suppose," muttered Bartram, who had been making intimate acquaintance with the black bottle above mentioned. "But watch, if you like, and call as many devils as you like! For my part, I shall be all the better for a snooze. Come, Joe!"

As the boy followed his father into the hut, he looked back at the wayfarer, and the tears came into his eyes; for his tender spirit had an intuition of the bleak and terrible loneliness in which this man had enveloped himself.

When they had gone Ethan Brand sat listening to the crackling of the kindled wood, and looking at the littlespirts of fire that issued through the chinks of the door. These trifles, however, once so familiar, had but the slightest hold of his attention, while deep within his mind he was reviewing the gradual but marvellous change that had been wrought upon him by the search to which he had devoted himself. He remembered how the night dew had fallen upon him,—how the dark forest had whispered to him,—how the stars had gleamed upon him,—a simple and loving man, watching his fire in the years gone by, and ever musing as it burned. He remembered with what tenderness, with what love and sympathy for mankind, and what pity for human guilt and woe, he had first begun to contemplate those ideas which afterwards became the inspiration of his life; with what reverence he had then looked into the heart of man, viewing it as a temple originally divine, and, however desecrated, still to be held sacred by a brother; with what awful fear he had deprecated the success of his pursuit, and prayed that the Unpardonable Sin might never be revealed to him. Then ensued that vast intellectual development, which in its progress disturbed the counterpoise between his mind and heart. The Idea that possessed his life had operated as a means of education; it had gone on cultivating his powers to the highest point of which they were susceptible; it had raised him from the level of an unlettered laborer to stand on a star-lit eminence, whither the philosophers of the earth, laden with the lore of universities, might vainly strive to clamber after him. So much for the intellect! But where was the heart? That, indeed, had withered,—had contracted,—had hardened,—had perished! It had ceased to partake of the universal throb. He had lost his hold of the magnetic chain of humanity. He was no longer a brother-man, opening the chambers or the dungeons of our common nature by the key of holy sympathy, which gave him a right to share in all its secrets; he was now a cold observer, looking on mankind as the subject of his experiment, and at length converting man and woman to be his puppets, and pulling the wires that moved them to such degrees of crime as were demanded for his study.

Thus Ethan Brand became a fiend. He began to be so from the moment that his moral nature had ceased to keep the pace of improvement with his intellect. And now, as his highest effort and inevitable development,—as the bright and gorgeous flower, and rich, delicious fruit of his life's labor,—he had produced the Unpardonable Sin!

"What more have I to seek? What more to achieve?" said Ethan Brand to himself. "My task is done, and well done!"

Starting from the log with a certain alacrity in his gait, and ascending the hillock of earth that was raised against the stone circumference of the lime-kiln, he thus reached the top of the structure. It was a space of perhaps ten feet across from edge to edge, presenting a view of the upper surface of the immense mass of broken marble with which the kiln was heaped. All these innumerable blocks and fragments of marble were red-hot and vividly on fire, sending up great spouts of blue flame, which quivered aloft and danced madly as within a magic circle, and sank and rose again with continual and multitudinous activity. As the lonely man bent forward over this terrible body of fire, the blasting heat smote up against his person with a breath that, it might be supposed, would have scorched and shrivelled him up in a moment.

Ethan Brand stood erect, and raised his arms on high. The blue flames played upon his face, and imparted the wild and ghastly light which alone could have suited its expression; it was that of a fiend on the verge of plunging into his gulf of intensest torment.

"O Mother Earth," cried he, "who art no more my Mother, and into whose bosom this frame shall never be resolved! O mankind, whose brotherhood I have cast off, and trampled thy great heart beneath my feet! O stars of heaven that shone on me of old, as if to light me onward and upward!—farewell all, and forever! Come, deadly element of Fire,—henceforth my familiar friend! Embrace me, as I do thee!"

That night the sound of a fearful peal of laughter rolled heavily through the sleep of the lime-burner and his little son; dim shapes of horror and anguish haunted their dreams, and seemed still present in the rude hovel when they opened their eyes to the daylight.

"Up, boy, up!" cried the lime-burner, staring about him. "Thank Heaven, the night is gone at last; and rather than pass such another, I would watch my lime-kiln, wide awake, for a twelvemonth. This Ethan Brand, with his humbug of an Unpardonable Sin, has done me no such mighty favor in taking my place!"

He issued from the hut, followed by little Joe, who kept fast hold of his father's hand. The early sunshine was already pouring its gold upon the mountain-tops;and though the valleys were still in shadow, they smiled cheerfully in the promise of the bright day that was hastening onward. The village, completely shut in by hills which swelled away gently about it, looked as if it had rested peacefully in the hollow of the great hand of Providence. Every dwelling was distinctly visible; the little spires of the two churches pointed upwards, and caught a fore-glimmering of brightness from the sun-gilt skies upon their gilded weathercocks. The tavern was astir, and the figure of the old smoke-dried stage-agent, cigar in mouth, was seen beneath the stoop. Old Graylock was glorified with a golden cloud upon his head. Scattered likewise over the breasts of the surrounding mountains, there were heaps of hoary mist in fantastic shapes, some of them far down into the valley, others high up towards the summits, and still others, of the same family of mist or cloud, hovering in the gold radiance of the upper atmosphere. Stepping from one to another of the clouds that rested on the hills, and thence to the loftier brotherhood that sailed in air, it seemed almost as if a mortal man might thus ascend into the heavenly regions. Earth was so mingled with sky that it was a day-dream to look at it.

To supply that charm of the familiar and homely, which Nature so readily adopts into a scene like this, the stage-coach was rattling down the mountain-road, and the driver sounded his horn, while echo caught up the notes, and intertwined them into a rich and varied and elaborate harmony, of which the original performer could lay claim to little share. The great hills played a concert among themselves, each contributing a strain of airy sweetness.

Little Joe's face brightened at once.

"Dear father," cried he, skipping cheerily to and fro, "that strange man is gone, and the sky and the mountains all seem glad of it!"

"Yes," growled the lime-burner, with an oath, "but he has let the fire go down, and no thanks to him if five hundred bushels of lime are not spoiled.

If I catch the fellow hereabouts again, I shall feel like tossing him into the furnace!"

With his long pole in his hand, he ascended to the top of the kiln. After a moment's pause, he called to his son.

"Come up here, Joe!" said he.

So little Joe ran up the hillock, and stood by his father's side. The marble was all burnt into perfect, snow-white lime. But on its surface, in the midst of the circle,—snow-white too, and thoroughly converted into lime,—lay a human skeleton, in the attitude of a person who, after long toil, lies down to long repose. Within the ribs—strange to say—was the shape of a human heart.

"Was the fellow's heart made of marble?" cried Bartram, in some perplexity at this phenomenon. "At any rate, it is burnt into what looks like special good lime; and, taking all the bones together, my kiln is half a bushel the richer for him."

So saying, the rude lime-burner lifted his pole, and, letting it fall upon the skeleton, the relics of Ethan Brand were crumbled into fragments.

THE SWANS OF LIR.

BY GERALD GRIFFIN.

After the battle of Tailltean, the Tuatha Danaans assembled together from the remotest corners of the five provinces of Ireland, in order to make arrangements for the future government of the isle. All agreed that it was better the whole country should be united under one monarch, chosen by common consent, than to continue subject to the interminable dissensions and oppressive imposts, arising from the rivalry of a number of petty sovereigns. Six candidates aspired to this supreme power, namely, Bogh Dearg, or Red Bow, of the tribe of the Deasies; Ibbreac, or the Many Colored, from the Red Stream; Lir; Fiuvar the Royal; Mioyar of the Great Burthen, so surnamed from his prodigious strength; and Aongusa Og, or young Oneas. All the rest of the Tuatha Danaans, except the six candidates, then went into council, and the determination was, to give the kingdom to Bogh Dearg, for three reasons. The first reason was, that his father had been a good man in his time; the second, that he was a good man himself; and the third, that he came of the best blood in the nation.

When Lir heard that the crown was to be given to Bogh Dearg, indignant at the choice, he returned to his own home, without waiting to see the new king inaugurated, or letting any of the assembly know that he was going, for he was convinced that the choice of the people would have fallen upon himself. Bogh Dearg, however, was proclaimed in due form, by the unanimous consent of the assembly, none of the five rejected candidates opposing his election, except Lir alone.

The ceremonies being concluded, the assembled tribes called on the new monarch to lead them in pursuit of Lir.

"Let us burn and spoil his territory," said they. "Why dares he, who never had a king in his family, presume to slight the sovereign we have chosen?"

"We will follow no such counsel," replied Bogh Dearg. "His ancestors and himself have always kept the province in which he lives in peace, and it will take nothing from my sovereignty over the Tuatha Danaans, to allow him still to hold his own possessions there."

The assembly, not fully satisfied with this reply, debated much on the course they had best take; but after much discussion, the question was allowed to rest for a time. Meanwhile an incident occurred which pressed heavily on the mind of Lir. His wife, whom he tenderly loved, fell ill and died in three nights. The report of her death, which was looked upon as a grievous loss in her own country, soon spread all over Ireland. It reached at length the ears of Bogh Dearg, and of the princes and nobles who were at his palace.

"Now," said the monarch, "if Lir were willing toaccede to it, I could propose a mode of redoubling the present friendship which I entertain for Lir. You all know that I have three daughters, the fairest in the kingdom, and I would praise them further, but that I am their father. I mean Aov, Aoife, and Alve, of whom Lir might choose which he pleased, to supply the place of his dead wife."

The speech of the king circulated amongst the Tuatha Danaans, and all agreed that a messenger ought to be sent to Lir in order to propose the connection, with a suitable dowry for the bride. When the ambassador arrived at the palace of Lir, he found the latter willing to accept the proposal, and, accordingly, both returned together to the royal residence of Bogh Dearg, on the shores of Lough Derg, where they were received on the part of the Tuatha Danaans with all the acclamations that even a more popular prince could expect. All parties seemed to take an interest in promoting the union.

The three daughters were sitting on chairs richly ornamented, in a hall of their father's palace. Near them sat the queen, wife of Bogh Dearg. When Lir and the monarch entered, the latter directed his attention to the three princesses, and bade him choose which he would.

"I do not know which of the three to choose," said Lir, "but the eldest is the most royal, and besides it is just that she should have precedence of the rest."

"Then," said the monarch, "that is Aov."

"Aov, then, I choose," replied Lir.

The marriage was celebrated with the magnificence becoming the rank of the parties. They remained a fortnight in the palace of the monarch, after which they went to the residence of Lir, who gave a splendid banquet on his arrival. In the progress of time Aov had twins, a son and a daughter, who were named, the one Fingula, and the other Aodh, or Eugene. In her next confinement, she gave birth to two sons, to whom were given the names of Fiacra and Cornu, but died herself, in a few days after. Lir was exceedingly grieved at her death, and, only for the love he bore his children, would almost have wished to die along with her. The tidings reached the monarch, who, together with all his household, made great lamentations for his eldest daughter, grieving more especially for the affliction which it caused to Lir.

"Nevertheless," said the monarch, "what has occurred need not dissolve the connection between Lir and us, for he can, if he please, take my second daughter, Aoife, to supply her place."

This speech, as was intended, soon found its way to Lir, who set out immediately for the palace of Bogh Dearg. The marriage was celebrated with the same splendor as on the former occasion, and Lir, after spending some time at the monarch's palace, returned to his house with Aoife, where he received her with all the love and honor which she could expect. For some time Aoife returned the same to him and to his children; and indeed any person who once saw those children could not avoid giving them all the love which any creature could receive. Frequently the old monarch came to see them to Lir'shouse, and often took them to his own, where he would gladly keep them, but that their father could not bear to have them out of his sight. It was the custom of the Tuatha Danaans to entertain each other in succession. When they assembled at the house of Lir, the four children were the whole subject of discourse, and the chief ornament of the day, they were so fair and so winning both in their appearances and their dispositions; and even as they dispersed to their several homes, the guests were heard to speak of nothing else. Lir himself would rise every morning at daybreak, and going to the apartment in which his children lay, would lie down among them for a while. The black poison of jealousy began at length to insinuate itself into the mind of Aoife. As if the love of Lir were not wide enough to comprehend them and herself, she conceived a mortal hatred against her sister's children. She feigned illness, and remained nearly a year in that condition, totally occupied in devising in her mind some means of ruining the children.

One morning she ordered her chariot, to the great surprise of Lir, who, however, was well pleased at this sign of returning health. Aoife next desired that the four children of Lir should be placed in the chariot with her, and drove away in the direction of Bogh Dearg's house. It was much against her will that Fingula, the daughter, went into the carriage, for she had long observed the increasing coolness in the mind of her step-mother, and guessed that she had no kindly purpose in her thoughts at present. She could not, however, avoid the destiny that was prepared for her, nor escape the suffering which she was doomed to undergo.

Aoife continued her journey until she arrived at Fiondach, where dwelt some of her father's people whom she knew to be deeply skilled in the art of the Druids. Having arrived at their residence, she went into the place where they were, and endeavored to prevail on them to kill the children, telling them that their father through his affection for them had slighted her, and promising to bestow on them all the riches which they could require.

"Ah," replied the Druids, "we would not kill the children of Lir for the whole world. You took an evil thought into your mind, and left your shame behind you, when you came with such a request to us."

"Then if you will not," cried Aoife, seizing a sword which lay near, "I will avenge myself, for I am resolved they shall not live."

Saying these words, she rushed out with the drawn sword, but through her womanhood she lost her courage when she was about to strike at the children. She then returned the sword to the Druids, and said she could not kill them.

Aoife resumed her journey, and they all drove on until they reached the shores of Lough Dairvreac, on the Lake of the Speckled Oak. Here she unharnessed the horses, and desired the children to descend and bathe in the lake. They did as she bade, but when all were in the water, she took a magic wand and struck them with it one after another. One after another the forms of the beautiful children disappeared, and four white swans were seen upon the water in their stead, when she addressed them in the following words:—

AOIFE.

Away, you children of the king! I have separated your lives from joy.

Your people will grieve to hear these tidings, but you shall continue birds.

What I have done, I have done through hatred of you, and malice to your father.

THE CHILDREN.

We, left here on the waters, must be tossed from wave to wave.

In the mean time Lir, returning to his palace, missed his children, and finding Aoife not yet come home, immediately guessed that she had destroyed them, for he likewise had observed her jealousy. In the morning he ordered his chariot to be prepared, and, following the track of his wife, travelled along until he came to the Lake of the Speckled Oak, when the children saw the chariot approaching, and Fingula spoke as follows:—

By yon old Oak, whose branches hoar

Wave o'er Lough Dairvreac's lonely shore,

Bright in the morn, a dazzling line

Of helms and silver targets shine;

Speed, brethren dear, speed towards the shelving strand,

'Tis royal Lir himself who leads the shining band.

Lir came to the brink of the water, and when he heard the birds conversing, as they drew nigh, in human language, he asked them how they became endowed with that surprising gift.

"Know, Lir," replied Fingula, "that we are your four children, who, through the frantic jealousy of ourstep-mother, and our own mother's sister, have been reduced to this unhappy condition."

"Are there any means," asked the wretched father, "by which you can ever be restored to your own forms again?"

"None," replied Fingula; "there is no man in existence able to effect that change, nor can it ever take place until a woman from the south, named Deocha, daughter of Ingri, the son of Black Hugh, and a man from the north, named Lairgnean, the son of Colman, shall occasion our deliverance in the time of THE TAILGEAN,[A] when the Christian faith and charity shall come into Ireland."

When Lir and his attendants heard these words, they uttered three doleful cries.

"Are you satisfied," said Lir, "since you retain your speech and reason, to come and remain with us?"

"It is not in our power to do so," replied Fingula, "nor are we at liberty to commit ourselves to the hands of man, until what I have told you shall have come to pass. But in the mean time we possess our speech and our mental faculties as fully as ever, and are moreover endowed with one additional quality, which is that we can sing the most melodious airs that the world has ever heard, and there is no mortal that would not feel a pleasure in listening to our voices. Remain with us for this night, and you shall hear our music."

When Lir had heard these words, he ordered hisfollowers to unharness their steeds, and they remained during the whole night on the strand, listening to the music of the birds, until all were lulled to sleep by the enchanting melody, excepting Lir alone. In the morning Lir arose from the bank on which he lay, and addressed his children in the following words:—

In vain I stretch my aching limbs

And close my weeping eyes,

In vain my children's moonlight hymns

For me alone arise.

'Tis morn again, on wave and strand,

My children, we must part;

A word that like a burning brand

Falls on your father's heart.

O had I seen this fatal hour,

When Lir's malignant queen

First sought his old paternal tower,

This hour had never been!

As thus between the shore and you

The widening waters grow,

So spreads my darkening spirits through

The sense of cureless woe.

Lir departed from the lake, and, still following the track of Aoife, came to the palace of the Ard-Righ, or Chief King, as Bogh Dearg was entitled. The monarch welcomed him, but complained of his not having brought his children as usual.

"Alas, poor that I am!" said Lir, "it is not I who would keep my children from your sight, but Aoife yonder, once your darling, and the sister of their mother,who has had them transformed into four swans, and abandoned them on the Lake of the Speckled Oak. They have been seen in that place by a great multitude of our people, who have heard the story from themselves, for they retain their speech and reason as before."

The monarch started at these words, and, looking on Aoife, immediately became convinced that Lir had spoken the truth. He began to upbraid his daughter in a rough and angry tone.

"Malicious as you were," said he, "you will suffer more by this cruel deed than the children of Lir, for they in the progress of time will be released from their sufferings, and their souls will be made happy in the end."

He then asked her into what shape of all living creatures she would least like to be transformed.

"Speak," said he, "for it is not in your power to avoid telling the truth."

Aoife, thus constrained, replied with a horrible look and tone, that there was no form which she more abhorred than that of a Deamhain Eidhir, or Demon of the Air.

"That form, then," said the monarch, "shall soon be yours"; and while he said so, he took a magic collar and laid it on her. Immediately losing her own shape, she flew away, shrieking, in that of a foul Spirit of the Air, in which she continues to this day, and will to the end of time, according to her deserts.

Soon afterwards, the monarch and the Tuatha Danaans went to the Lake of the Speckled Oak and encamped upon its shores, listening to the music of the birds. The Sons of Mile, likewise, came thither from every part ofIreland, and formed an encampment in the same place, for there never was music comparable to that of those swans. Sometimes they related their mournful story, sometimes they would answer the questions proposed to them by the people on shore, and talk familiarly with their relatives and friends, and at others they sung, both by day and night, the most delightful music that was ever heard by human ear; so that the listeners on shore, notwithstanding the grief and uneasiness in which they continued, enjoyed as sweet sleep, and arose as fresh and vigorous, as if they had been resting in their accustomed beds at home. The two multitudes of the Sons of Mile, and of the Tuatha Danaans, thus remained in their respective encampments during the space of thirty years. At the end of that time, Fingula addressed her brethren as follows:—

"Are you ignorant, my brothers, that but one night is left of the time which you were to spend upon the lake?"

On hearing this, the three brethren grew very sorrowful, and uttered many plaintive cries and sounds of grief; for they were almost as happy on that lake, enjoying the company of their friends and relatives, talking with them and answering their questions, as they would have been in their own home; more especially, when compared to the grief they felt on leaving it for the wild and stormy sea that lies to the north of Ireland. Early in the morning they came as close to the brink of the lake as they could, and spoke to their father and their friends, to all of whom they bade a mournful farewell, repeating those pitiful lines that follow:—

Receive, O royal sage, our last farewell,

Thou of the potent spell!

And thou, O Lir, deep skilled in mystic lore—

We meet—we meet no more!

The sum complete of our appointed hours,

We leave your happy bowers.

Farewell, dear friends, till time itself is o'er

We meet, we meet no more!

Forever now to human converse lost,

On Moyle's wild waters tost,

Our doom till day, and night, and seasons fail,

To weave a mournful tale.

Three lingering ages on the northern main

To waste in various pain.

Three lingering ages in the stormy west

To heave on ocean's breast.

Sad is our doom, dear friends, on wintry seas

Through many a year to freeze,—

Harsh brine and rocks, with horrid sea-weed brown

For Lir's soft beds of down!

No more the joy of Lir's paternal breast,

Early we part unblest!

A power unseen commands that we forsake

Lone Dairvreac's peaceful lake.

Rise from the wave, companions of my fear,

Rise, brethren dear!

Bright wave and pebbly beach and echoing dell,

Farewell, a last farewell!

And you, dear friends, who throng the leafy shore,

We meet—we meet no more!

Having ended those verses, the swans took wing and, arising lightly on the air, continued their flight until theyreached the Sruih na Maoile, or the Sea of Moyle, as those waters were called which flowed between Ireland and Scotland. Their departure occasioned deep sorrow to all who witnessed it, and they had a law proclaimed throughout the kingdom, that any one, from the king to the peasant, who should kill a swan, let his power be as great as it might, should meet with certain death. In the mean time, the children of Lir found that they had made an unhappy change of place. When they saw the broad wild ocean around them, they grew cold and hungry, and began to fall into despair, thinking that all they ever suffered was nothing until they were sent to these seas. They remained on the waters until one night it began to freeze very hard.

"My loving brothers," said Fingula, "we make very unwise provision against the coming night if we do not keep close together; and lest by any mischance we should lose sight of each other, let us appoint a place where we may meet again as soon as it may be in our power."

"In that case, dear sister," said the three brothers, "let us meet at the Carrig na Roin (or the Rock of the Seals), for that is a place with which we are all acquainted."

They continued thus until about the middle of the night. The wind then increased to a storm, the waters arose, and the mountains of brine as they rolled and broke around them sparkled in the gloom as if they had taken fire. So great was the tempest that the children of Lir were separated by the waves. All were scattered far and wide, nor could one tell whither any of the three others had been driven. At length it abated a little of its violence, the deep became more settled, and Fingula found herself alone. Not being able to see her brethren anywhere around, she felt the deepest anxiety of mind, and at length broke forth into the following words:—

Heart-broken o'er these seas I glide,

My frozen wings together clinging:

No more along the stormy tide

I hear my brethren singing.

Three lingering ages, marked by woes,

Since first we left Lone Dairvreac's water

Break, break, my heart, and give repose

To Lir's unhappy daughter.

Beloved alike, O loved so well,

That made your sister's breast your pillow.

Tell me, my wandering brethren, tell,

Where roam you o'er the billow?

Hid by what rocks or secret caves,

That wont beneath my wings to slumber,

I fear the dead will leave their graves,

Ere time restore our number.

Tossed by the surge and sleety storm

At random o'er this briny water;

Woe, woe to all who share the form

Of Lir's unhappy daughter.

Fingula remained that night on the Rock of the Seals. At sunrise the next morning, looking out in every direction along the water, she saw Cornu coming towardsher with head drooping, and feathers drenched with spray, so cold and feeble that he could not answer her questions. Fingula received him lovingly under her wings, and said:—

"If Eugene were with us now, our condition would be tolerable."

Not long after she saw Eugene coming towards her, with a drooping head, and wings hanging to the ground, and she welcomed him, and put him under the feathers of her breast. Immediately after she saw Fiacra approaching, and she then removed Cornu from beneath her right wing and placed him under her left, and put Fiacra beneath her right wing, where Cornu had been before. She then settled her feathers about them, and said:—

"Severe, my dear brothers, as you have found the last night, you must yet see many more as bad."

The children of Lir continued for a long time in the same condition on the Sruih na Maoile, until one night they suffered so much from the cold and wind and snow, that nothing they had hitherto felt was comparable to it; which made Fingula utter the following words:—

Hard is our life and sharp with ill,

My brethren dear;

The snow so thick, the wind so chill,

The night so drear.

We strive to keep

Sad concert in our songs of pain,

But the wild deep,

Relentless, mars the rising strain.

Vainly we soothe our aching hearts

With converse sweet,

Wave after wave, high heaving, parts

Our union meet.

Ah, doom severe!

Harsh was our mother's vengeful will,

Ah, brethren dear,

Hard is our life, and sharp with ill.

They remained for a year on the Sea of Moyle, when one night, as they were on the Rock of the Seals, the waters congealed around them with the cold; and as they lay on the rock, their feet and wings were frozen to it, so that they could not move a limb. When at length, after using what strength remained in their bodies, they succeeded in getting free, the skin of their feet, and the innermost down of their breasts, and the quills of their wings, remained clinging to the icy crag.

"Woe to the children of Lir!" said Fingula, "mournful is our fate to-night, for when the salt water pierces into our wounds, we shall be pained to death"; and she sung these lines:—

Sad is our hap this mournful night,

With mangled feet and plumage bleeding;

Our wings no more sustain our flight,

Woe comes to linked woe succeeding.

Ah, cruel was our step-dame's mind,

When hard to nature's sweet emotion,

She sent us here 'mid wave and wind,

To freeze on Moyle's relentless ocean.

The wild sea-foam that strews the shore,

The weeds those briny waves engender,

For past delights are all our store,

Though fostered once in regal splendor.

Rise, sister of three brethren dear,

Let custom dull the edge of anguish,

In hollow rock or cavern drear,

By doom unrighteous, bound to languish.

Leaving the Rock of the Seals, they alighted again on the waters of Moyle, where the sharp brine pierced them keenly, although they strove to keep their feet under their wings as closely as they could. They continued to suffer thus, until their feathers grew, and the wounds of their feet were healed. They used frequently to go as near the shore as they could, on that part of the Irish coast which looks towards Scotland, and every night they came together to Moyle, which was their constant place of rest. One day as they drew nigh the shore of Bama, to the north, they saw a number of chariots and horsemen, splendidly arrayed, with horses richly caparisoned, approaching from the west.

"Do you observe that brilliant company, you sons of Lir?" said Fingula.

"We know not who they are," replied her brethren, "but they seem to be Irish; whether of the Sons of Mile, or the Tuatha Danaans, it is impossible for us to conjecture."

They drew close to the shore, in order to observe more accurately. When the horsemen saw them coming, they hastened towards them, until they came within speaking distance. The persons of note who were amongst them were Aodh Aithiosatch, or Merry Hugh, and Feargus Fithcall (of the Complete Armor), the two sons of BoghDearg the Monarch, and the third part of his bodyguard. The children of Lir inquired how the Tuatha Danaans were, and especially Lir and Bogh Dearg, with their friends and dependants.

"They are all well in their respective homes," replied the horsemen. "At present, it is true, they are in your father's palace, partaking of a splendid banquet, in health and joy, knowing no other want than that of your absence, and their ignorance of your place of abode, since you left the Lake of the Speckled Oak."

"Evil has been our life since then," said Fingula, "for neither we nor any other creature, that we have heard of, ever suffered so much as we have done, since we came to the waters of Moyle"; and she uttered the following words:—

We four are well,

Though in keen want and sombre grief we dwell.

Happy are they

Who sit in Lir's bright hall, and share his banquet gay.

Rich food and wine

For them in sparkling gold and silver shine;

While far away

His children shiver in the hungry spray!

We, who of yore

On dainties fared, and silken garments wore,

Now all our fare,

Cold sand, and bitter brine, for wax and honey rare;

Our softest bed,

The crag that o'er those surges lifts its head;

Oft have we laid

Our limbs on beds of tenderest down arrayed.

Now must we lie,

On Moyle's rough wave, with plumage seldom dry;

A pageant rare

Oft bore us to our grandsire's palace fair.

Ah, mournful change!

Now with faint wings these dreary shores I range.

O'er Moyle's dark tide,

Plume touching plume, we wander side by side;

Sharing no more

The joys that cheered our happy hearts of yore;

The welcome mild,

That on our grandsire's kingly features smiled;

Lir's counsel meet,

And fond paternal kiss, that made the morning sweet.

The horsemen returned soon after to the house of Lir, and told the principal men of the Tuatha Danaans where they had seen the birds, and the dialogue they had held together.

"We cannot assist them," they replied, "but we are well pleased to hear that they live, for they will be restored to their former shape, after a long time has elapsed."

The children of Lir, meantime, returned northwards to the Sea of Moyle, where they remained until their time in that place had expired. Then Fingula spoke to her brothers, and said:—

"It is time for us to depart from hence, for the period appointed for us to remain here is at an end"; and she added these verses:—

At length we leave this cheerless shore,

Unblest by summer's sunshine splendid;

Its storm for us shall howl no more,

Our time on gloomy Moyle is ended.

Three hundred sunless summers past,

We leave at length this loveless billow;

Where oft we felt the icy blast,

And made the shelving crag our pillow.

Still on our lingering night of pain,

Far distant beams the dawn of gladness;

Light ease beside the western main

Awaits our long accustomed sadness.

Long must we haunt that billowy shore,

Ere breaks for us the daybeam splendid,

But here our numbered years are o'er,

Our time on gloomy Moyle is ended.

After that time the children of Lir left the Sea of Moyle, and flew until they came to the most westerly part of the ocean. They were there for a long time, suffering all kinds of hardship, until they happened to see a man, a tiller of the ground, who used often to watch them when they came near the shore, and took great pleasure in listening to their music. He told the people on the coast of what he had seen, and spread the tidings of the prodigy far and near. However, the same tale remains to be repeated, for the children of Lir never suffered so much before or after as they did on that very night, after the husbandman had seen them; the frost was so keen, and the snow coming so thick upon the wind. The waters all congealed into ice, so that the woods and the sea were of one color. Their feet stuck to the ground, leaving them unable to move, and they began to utter the most lamentable cries, while Fingulacomforted, and strove to persuade them not to grieve, but in vain; and she repeated these lines:—

Sad are my suffering brethren's piercing cries,

This dreary night!

Sharp drives the snow shower, o'er the moonless skies,

With ceaseless flight!

Where'er they search the frost-bound ocean o'er,

On solid ice their thirsty beaks are ringing,

Nor on the wintry shore

Fresh water laves their plumes, nor bubbling fount is springing.

O thou dread Monarch, who to sea and coast

Their being gave,

And led'st, as shadowy rumor tells, a host,

Through the deep wave!

Behold these wretched birds with pitying eyes,

Their lingering years in joyless slavery spending,

In thy great might arise,

And bid our souls be free, their bonds of anguish rending.

"Brothers," said Fingula, "confide in Him who made heaven, and the elements, the earth with all its fruit, and the sea with all its wonders, and you will find comfort and relief."

"We do confide in him," they answered.

"And I confide with you," said Fingula, "in the only being who is full of knowledge and of pity." They remained on the Oraas Domhnan (Deep Seas) until their time was fulfilled, when Fingula said:—

"It is time for us to go to Fioncha, where Lir and his people dwell, and our people also."

"We are well content to do so," replied they; andall proceeded together somewhat joyfully, until they came to Fioncha. They found the place where their father's palace had stood, and all around it, without either house or inhabitants, but everything looking dreary and dull. They saw smoke at a distance, and the four came towards it, and uttered three mournful cries, and Fingula repeated these words:—

A mournful wonder is this place to me,

Which once I knew so well!

Not even the trace of that loved home I see,

Where Lir was wont to dwell.

Nor hound, nor steed, nor lord nor lady bright,

Nor welcome spoken!

Since I have lived to see this mournful sight,

My heart is broken.

This was not in our father's time of old,

A loveless, lightless waste,

Without a cup the sparkling wine to hold,

Or princely guest to taste.

The home where oft we hailed each joyous morn

Is bleak and lonely!

And nothing left to us, its heirs forlorn,

Save memory only.

Now do I know the deep devouring grave

Holds all who once were dear!

Sad was our life on Moyle's tempestuous wave,

But keener grief is here.

Low rustling grass, and winds that sadly blow

Through dry leaves creeping!

And he who should his cherished darlings know,

Forever sleeping!

The children of Lir remained in the place where their father and their ancestors had lived, and where they had themselves been nursed and educated, and late at night they began to sing most melodious music. In the morning they took wing and flew until they came to Inis Gluaire Breanain, and they began to sing there; so that all the birds of the country that could swim came to that place, which was called Lochan na Heanlaithe (or the Lake of the Birds). They continued in that condition for a long time, until the Christian doctrine was preached in those countries, when St. Patrick came to Ireland, and St. Macaomh Og came to Inis Gluaire Breanain. The first night he came there the children of Lir heard the sound of the bell ringing near them, and were greatly rejoiced. They hastened towards the place from whence they heard the bells, and the three sons of Lir made such speed that they left Fingula by herself.

"What is the matter with you, dear brethren?" said Fingula.

"We cannot tell," they replied, "we know not how to account for the heavenly music we have heard."

"I will explain it to you," said she; "that is the bell of Macaomh Og, and it is by him you shall be released from your pain and trouble, and you shall be comforted"; and she said these lines:—

List, list to the sound of the anchoret's bell,

Rise, children of Lir, from the wave where ye dwell,

Uplift your glad wings and exult as ye hear,

And give thanks, for the hour of your freedom is near.

He merits our duty, the Mighty to save

From the rock and the surge, from the storm and the wave.

Who clings to his doctrine with constant endeavor,

His grief shall be turned into glory forever.

Past moments of anguish, forever farewell!

List, children of Lir, to the sound of the bell.

The children of Lir were listening to the music of the bell until the saint had finished his prayers.

"Let us now," said Fingula, "sing our own music to the great Ruler of the heavens and the earth"; and they sung the most melodious strains of praise and adoration. Macaomh Og was listening, and in the morning early he came to the Lake of the Birds. Coming close to the shore, he asked them, were they the children of Lir?

"We are, indeed," they answered.

"I am most thankful to hear it," said he, "for it was to relieve you that I was sent to this island, rather than to any other part of Ireland."

On hearing these words the children of Lir came to the shore, and depended on his word. He took them down to his residence, where they remained listening to his instructions and joining in his devotions day after day. Macaomh Og sent for a craftsman and desired him to make two silver chains, which he accordingly did. One of them he put between Eugene and Fingula, and the other between Cornu and Fiacra.

The king who governed Conact at that time was named Lairgnean, the son of Colman (the same of whom Fingula had spoken to her father on the Lake of the Speckled Oak), and his queen's name was Deocha, the daughter of Ingri, son of Black Hugh. Deocha came to hear of the wonderful birds, and, being seized with a violent desire of possessing them, requested the king to procure them forher. He replied that he could never persuade himself to ask Macaomh Og to give them up. Deocha, enraged at his refusal, declared that she never again would spend a night within the palace of Glairgnea, as the king's residence was called, unless she got the swans; and, leaving the palace, she travelled to Kill da Luadh (now called Killaloe) and took up her abode at her own home. When Lairgnean found her so resolute, he sent a messenger three several times for the birds, but could not obtain them. Then he came himself to Macaomh Og, and asked him if it were true he had refused his messengers.

"It is true," answered Macaomh Og.

"Then," said the king, "it is true, likewise, that I will take them with me whether you are willing or otherwise."

As he said this he rushed toward the altar near which they stood, and seized the two chains which coupled them together. No sooner had he done so, than the swans lost their plumage, their beautiful feathers disappeared, and the three sons of Lir appeared three withered old men, with their bones seeming to project through their skin; while Fingula, instead of the graceful swan that sung such enchanting strains, became an old shrivelled hag, fleshless and bloodless. The King let fall the chains, and returned home, while Macaomh Og uttered many lamentations after the birds, and pronounced a malediction on Lairgnean. Fingula then said:—

"Come hither, holy father, and give us baptism, for we are as much concerned at parting with you as you in parting with us. You are to bury us together in this manner. Place Cornu and Fiacra at my back, and placeEugene before me"; and she again said, "Baptize us, holy father, and make us happy."

After that they departed this life, and the children of Lir were buried by Macaomh Og as Fingula had desired. He raised the earth in the form of a tomb, and placed a stone over them, on which he carved their names in the Ogham character, and wept bitterly above their grave. It is thought that their souls went to heaven. For Lairgnean, who was the immediate cause of their death, Macaomh Og predicted his fate in the following lines:—

Ill shoot of Colman's royal line,

The malison of heaven is thine,

The grief which thou hast caused to mine,

Thine own cold heart shall feel,

Thou whose unholy zeal

Hath left me on this isle forlorn,

My cherished darlings' loss to mourn.

And she whose soul, in evil strong,

Hath prompted this unfeeling wrong,

To early dust consigned, shall long

Her fruitless rapine wail,

A shivering spectre pale!

The malison of heaven is thine,

Ill shoot of Colman's royal line!

Not long after, Lairgnean and his wife died a sudden death, according to the prediction of Macaomh Og, which concludes the history of the Swans of Lir.

A NIGHT IN A WORKHOUSE.

BY JAMES GREENWOOD.

At about nine o'clock on the evening of Monday the —th instant, a neat but unpretentious carriage might have been seen turning cautiously from the Kennington Road into Princes Road, Lambeth. The curtains were closely drawn, and the coachman wore an unusually responsible air. Approaching a public house, which retreated a little from the street, he pulled up; but not so close that the lights should fall upon the carriage door, not so distant as to unsettle the mind of any one who chose to imagine that he had halted to drink beer before proceeding to call for the children at a juvenile party. He did not dismount, nor did any one alight in the usual way; but any keen observer who happened to watch his intelligent countenance might have seen a furtive glance directed to the wrong door,—that is to say, to the door of the carriage which opened into the dark and muddy road. From that door emerged a sly and ruffianly figure, marked with every sign of squalor. He was dressed in what had once been a snuff-browncoat, but which had faded to the hue of bricks imperfectly baked. It was not strictly a ragged coat, though it had lost its cuffs,—a bereavement which obliged the wearer's arms to project through the sleeves two long inelegant inches. The coat altogether was too small, and was only made to meet over the chest by means of a bit of twine. This wretched garment was surmounted by a "bird's-eye" pocket-handkerchief of cotton, wisped about the throat hangman fashion; above all was a battered billy-cock hat, with a dissolute drooping brim. Between the neckerchief and the lowering brim of the hat appeared part of a face, unshaven, and not scrupulously clean. The man's hands were plunged into his pockets, and he shuffled hastily along in boots, which were the boots of a tramp indifferent to miry ways. In a moment he was out of sight, and the brougham, after waiting a little while, turned about and comfortably departed.

This mysterious figure was that of the present writer. He was bound for Lambeth Workhouse, there to learn by actual experience how casual paupers are lodged and fed, and what the "casual" is like, and what the porter who admits him, and the master who rules over him; and how the night passes with the outcasts whom we have all seen crowding about workhouse doors on cold and rainy nights. Much has been said on the subject,—on behalf of the paupers, on behalf of the officials; but nothing by any one who, with no motive but to learn and make known the truth, had ventured the experiment of passing a night in a workhouse and trying what it actually is to be a "casual."

The day had been windy and chill,—the night wascold; and therefore I fully expected to begin my experiences among a dozen of ragged wretches squatting about the steps and waiting for admission. But my only companion at the door was a decently dressed woman, whom, as I afterwards learnt, they declined to admit until she had recovered from a fit of intoxication from which she had the misfortune to be still suffering. I lifted the big knocker and knocked; the door was promptly opened, and I entered. Just within, a comfortable-looking clerk sat at a comfortable desk, ledger before him. Indeed, the spacious hall in every way was as comfortable as cleanliness and great mats and plenty of gaslight could make it.

"What do you want?" asked the man who opened the door.

"I want a lodging."

"Go and stand before the desk," said the porter; and I obeyed.

"You are late," said the clerk.

"Am I, sir?"

"Yes. If you come in you'll have a bath, and you'll have to sleep in the shed."

"Very well, sir."

"What's your name?"

"Joshua Mason, sir."

"What are you?"

"An engraver." (This taradiddle I invented to account for the look of my hands.)

"Where did you sleep last night?"

"Hammersmith," I answered—as I hope to be forgiven.

"How many times have you been here?"

"Never before, sir."

"Where do you mean to go to when you are turned out in the morning?"

"Back to Hammersmith, sir."

These humble answers being entered in a book, the clerk called to the porter, saying, "Take him through. You may as well take his bread with you."

Near the clerk stood a basket containing some pieces of bread of equal size. Taking one of these, and unhitching a bunch of keys from the wall, the porter led me through some passages all so scrupulously clean that my most serious misgivings were laid to rest. Then we passed into a dismal yard. Crossing this, my guide led me to a door, calling out, "Hillo! Daddy, I've brought you another!" Whereupon Daddy opened unto us, and let a little of his gaslight stream into the dark where we stood.

"Come in," said Daddy, very hospitably. "There's enough of you to-night, anyhow! What made you so late?"

"I didn't like to come in earlier."

"Ah! that's a pity, now, because you've missed your skilley (gruel). It's the first night of skilley, don't you know, under the new Act?"

"Just like my luck!" I muttered dolefully.

The porter went his way, and I followed Daddy into another apartment, where were ranged three great baths, each one containing a liquid so disgustingly like weak mutton broth that my worst apprehensions crowded back. "Come on, there's a dry place to stand on up at thisend," said Daddy, kindly. "Take off your clothes, tie 'em up in your hank'sher, and I'll lock 'em up till the morning." Accordingly I took off my coat and waistcoat, and was about to tie them together, when Daddy cried, "That ain't enough; I mean everything." "Not my shirt, sir, I suppose?" "Yes, shirt and all; but there, I'll lend you a shirt," said Daddy. "Whatever you take in of your own will be nailed, you know. You might take in your boots, though,—they'd be handy if you happened to want to leave the shed for anything; but don't blame me if you lose 'em."

With a fortitude for which I hope some day to be rewarded, I made up my bundle (boots and all), and the moment Daddy's face was turned away shut my eyes and plunged desperately into the mutton broth. I wish from the bottom of my heart my courage had been less hasty, for hearing the splash, Daddy looked round and said, "Lor, now! there was no occasion for that; you look a clean and decent sort of man. It's them filthy beggars" (only he used a word more specific than "filthy") "that want washing. Don't use that towel: here's a clean one! That's the sort! and now here's your shirt" (handing me a blue striped one from a heap), "and here's your ticket. No. 34 you are, and a ticket to match is tied to your bundle. Mind you don't lose it. They'll nail it from you if they get a chance. Put it under your head. This is your rug: take it with you."

"Where am I to sleep, please, sir?"

"I'll show you."

And so he did. With no other rag but the checked shirt to cover me, and with my rug over my shoulder,he accompanied me to the door at which I entered, and, opening it, kept me standing with naked feet on the stone threshold, full in the draught of the frosty air, while he pointed out the way I should go. It was not a long way, but I would have given much not to have trodden it. It was open as the highway,—with flag-stones below and the stars overhead, and, as I said before, and cannot help saying again, a frosty wind was blowing.

"Straight across," said Daddy, "to where you see the light shining through. Go in there, and turn to the left, and you'll find the beds in a heap. Take one of 'em and make yourself comfortable." And straight across I went, my naked feet seeming to cling to the stones as though they were burning hot instead of icy cold (they had just stepped out of a bath you should remember), till I reached the space through which the light was shining, and I entered in.

No language with which I am acquainted is capable of conveying an adequate conception of the spectacle I then encountered. Imagine a space of about thirty feet by thirty feet enclosed on three sides by a dingy whitewashed wall, and roofed with naked tiles, which were furred with the damp and filth that reeked within. As for the fourth side of the shed, it was boarded in for (say) a third of its breadth; the remaining space being hung with flimsy canvas, in which was a gap two feet wide at top, widening to at least four feet at bottom. This far too airy shed was paved with stone, the flags so thickly incrusted with filth that I mistook it first for a floor of natural earth. Extending from one end of my bedroom to the other, in three rows, were certain iron"cranks" (of which I subsequently learnt the use), with their many arms raised in various attitudes, as the stiffened arms of men are on a battle-field. My bedfellows lay among the cranks, distributed over the flag-stones in a double row, on narrow bags scantily stuffed with hay. At one glance my appalled vision took in thirty of them,— thirty men and boys stretched upon shallow pallets, with but only six inches of comfortable hay between them and the stony floor. These beds were placed close together, every occupant being provided with a rug like that which I was fain to hug across my shoulders. In not a few cases two gentlemen had clubbed beds and rugs and slept together. In one case (to be further mentioned presently) four gentlemen had so clubbed together. Many of my fellow-casuals were awake,—others asleep or pretending to sleep; and shocking as were the waking ones to look upon, they were quite pleasant when compared with the sleepers. For this reason, the practised and well-seasoned casual seems to have a peculiar way of putting himself to bed. He rolls himself in his rug, tucking himself in, head and feet, so that he is completely enveloped; and, lying quite still on his pallet, he looks precisely like a corpse covered because of its hideousness. Some were stretched out at full length; some lay nose and knees together; some with an arm or a leg showing crooked through the coverlet. It was like the result of a railway accident; these ghastly figures were awaiting the coroner.

From the moral point of view, however, the wakeful ones were more dreadful still. Tousled, dirty, villanous, they squatted up in their beds, and smoked foul pipes,and sang snatches of horrible songs, and bandied jokes so obscene as to be absolutely appalling. Eight or ten were so enjoying themselves,—the majority with the check shirt on, and the frowzy rug pulled about their legs; but two or three wore no shirts at all, squatting naked to the waist, their bodies fully exposed in the light of the single flaring jet of gas fixed high up on the wall.

My entrance excited very little attention. There was a horse-pail three parts full of water standing by a post in the middle of the shed, with a little tin pot beside it. Addressing me as "old pal," one of the naked ruffians begged me to "hand him a swig," as he was "werry nigh garspin." Such an appeal of course no "old pal" could withstand, and I gave him a potful of water. He showed himself grateful for the attention. "I should lay over there, if I was you," he said, pointing to the left side of the shed; "it's more out of the wind than this 'ere side is." I took the good-natured advice, and (by this time shivering with cold) stepped over the stones to where the beds of straw-bags were heaped, and dragged one of them to the spot suggested by my naked comrade. But I had no more idea of how to arrange it than of making an apple-pudding; and a certain little discovery added much to my embarrassment. In the middle of the bed I had selected was a stain of blood bigger than a man's hand! I did not know what to do now. To lie on such a horrid thing seemed impossible; yet to carry back the bed and exchange it for another might betray a degree of fastidiousness repugnant to the feelings of my fellow-lodgers, and possibly excite suspicion that I was not what I seemed. Just in the nick of time in came that good man Daddy.

"What! not pitched yet?" he exclaimed; "here, I'll show you. Hallo! somebody's been a bleedin'! Never mind; let's turn him over. There you are, you see! Now lay down, and cover your rug over you."

There was no help for it. It was too late to go back. Down I lay and spread the rug over me. I should have mentioned that I brought in with me a cotton handkerchief, and this I tied round my head by way of a nightcap; but not daring to pull the rug as high as my face. Before I could in any way settle my mind to reflection, in came Daddy once more to do me a further kindness and point out a stupid blunder I had committed.

"Why, you are a rummy chap!" said Daddy. "You forgot your bread! Lay hold. And look here, I've brought you another rug; it's perishing cold to-night." So saying he spread the rug over my legs and went away. I was very thankful for the extra covering, but I was in a dilemma about the bread. I couldn't possibly eat it; what then was to be done with it? I broke it, however, and in view of such of the company as might happen to be looking, made a ferocious bite at a bit as large as a bean, and munched violently. By good luck, however, I presently got half-way over my difficulty very neatly. Just behind me, so close indeed that their feet came within half a yard of my head, three lads were sleeping together.

"Did you hear that, Punch?" one of them asked.

"'Ear what?" answered Punch, sleepy and snappish.

"Why, a cove forgot his toke! Gordstruth! you wouldn't ketch me a forgettin' mine."

"You may have half of it, old pal, if you're hungry", I observed, leaning upon my elbows.

"Chuck it here, good luck to yer!" replied my young friend, starting up with an eager clap of his dirty hands.

I "chucked it here," and slipping the other half under the side of my bed, lay my head on my folded arms.

It was about half past nine when, having made myself as comfortable as circumstances permitted, I closed my eyes in the desperate hope that I might fall asleep, and so escape from the horrors with which I was surrounded. "At seven to-morrow morning the bell will ring," Daddy had informed me, "and then you will give up your ticket and get back your bundle." Between that time and the present full nine long hours had to wear away.

But I was speedily convinced that, at least for the present, sleep was impossible. The young fellow (one of the three who lay in one bed, with their feet to my head) whom my bread had refreshed, presently swore with frightful imprecations that he was now going to have a smoke; and immediately put his threat into execution. Thereupon his bedfellows sat up and lit their pipes too. But O, if they had only smoked,—if they had not taken such an unfortunate fancy to spit at the leg of a crank, distant a few inches from my head,—how much misery and apprehension would have been spared me. To make matters worse, they united with this American practice an Eastern one; as they smoked they related little autobiographical anecdotes,—so abominable that three or four decent men who lay at the farther end of the shed were so provoked that they threatened, unless the talk abated in filthiness, to get up and stop it by main force.Instantly the voice of every blackguard in the room was raised against the decent ones.

They were accused of loathsome afflictions, stigmatized "as fighting men out of work" (which must be something very humiliating, I suppose), and invited to "a round" by boys young enough to be their grandsons. For several minutes there was such a storm of oaths, threats, and taunts,—such a deluge of foul words raged in the room,—that I could not help thinking of the fate of Sodom; as, indeed, I did several times during the night. Little by little the riot died out, without any the slightest interference on the part of the officers.

Soon afterwards the ruffian majority was strengthened by the arrival of a lanky boy of about fifteen, who evidently, recognized many acquaintances, and was recognized by them as "Kay," or perhaps I should write it "K." He was a very remarkable-looking lad, and his appearance pleased me much. Short as his hair was cropped, it still looked soft and silky; he had large blue eyes, set wide apart, and a mouth that would have been faultless but for its great width; and his voice was as soft and sweet as any woman's. Lightly as a woman, too, he picked his way over the stones towards the place where the beds lay, carefully hugging his cap beneath his arm.

"What cheer, Kay?" "Out again, then, old son!" "What yer got in yer cap, Kay?" cried his friends; to which the sweet voice replied, "Who'll give me a part of his doss (bed)? —— my —— eyes and limbs if I ain't perishin'! Who'll let me turn in with him for half my toke (bread)?" I feared how it would be! The hungry young fellow who had so readily availed himself ofhalf my "toke" snapped at Kay's offer, and after a little rearrangement and bed-making, four young fellows instead of three reposed upon the hay-bags at my head.

"You was too late for skilley, Kay. There's skilley now, nights as well as mornin's."

"Don't you tell no bleeding lies," Kay answered, incredulously.

"Blind me, it's true. Ain't it, Punch?"

"Right you are!" said Punch, "and spoons to eat it with, that's more! There used to be spoons at all the houses, one time. Poplar used to have 'em; but one at a time they was all nicked, don't you know." ("Nicked" means "stolen," obviously.)

"Well, I don't want no skilley, leastways, not to-night," said Kay. "I've had some rum. Two glasses of it; and a blow out of puddin',—regler Christmas plum-puddin'. You don't know the cove as give it me, but, thinks I this mornin' when I come out, blessed if I don't go and see my old chum. Lordstruth! he was struck! 'Come along,' he ses, 'I saved you some puddin' from Christmas.' 'Whereabouts is it?' I ses. 'In that box under my bed,' he ses, and he forks it out. That's the sort of pal to have! And he stood a quarten, and half a ounce of hard-up (tobacco). That wasn't all, neither; when I come away, ses he, 'How about your breakfus?' 'O, I shall do,' ses I. 'You take some of my bread and butter,' he ses, and he cuts me off four chunks buttered thick. I eat two on 'em comin' along."

"What's in your cap, Kay?" repeated the devourer of "toke."

"Them other two slices," said Kay; generously adding,"There, share 'em amongst yer, and somebody give us a whiff of 'bacca."

Kay showed himself a pleasant companion,—what in a higher grade of society is called "quite an acquisition." He told stories of thieves and thieving, and of a certain "silver cup" he had been "put up to," and that he meant to nick it afore the end of the week, if he got seven stretch (? seven years) for it. The cup was worth ten quid (? pounds), and he knew where to melt it within ten minutes of nicking it. He made this statement without any moderation of his sweet voice; and the others received it as serious fact. Nor was there any affectation of secrecy in another gentleman, who announced, with great applause, that he had stolen a towel from the bath-room; "And s' help me, it's as good as new; never been washed mor'n once!"

"Tell us a 'rummy' story, Kay," said somebody; and Kay did. He told stories of so "rummy" a character that the decent men at the farther end of the room (some of whom had their own little boys sleeping with them) must have lain in a sweat of horror as they listened. Indeed, when Kay broke into a "rummy" song with a roaring chorus, one of the decent men rose in his bed and swore that he would smash Kay's head if he didn't desist. But Kay sang on till he and his admirers were tired of the entertainment. "Now," said he, "let's have a swearing club! you'll all be in it?"

The principle of this game seemed to rest on the impossibility of either of the young gentlemen making half a dozen observations without introducing a blasphemous or obscene word; and either the basis is a very soundone, or for the sake of keeping the "club" alive the members purposely made slips. The penalty for "swearing" was a punch on any part of the body, except a few which the club rules protected. The game was highly successful. Warming with the sport, and indifferent to punches, the members vied with each other in audacity; and in a few minutes Bedlam in its prime could scarcely have produced such a spectacle as was to be seen on the beds behind me. One rule of the club was that any word to be found in the Bible might be used with impunity, and if one member "punched" another for using such a word, the error was to be visited upon him with a double punching all round. This naturally led to much argument; for in vindicating the Bible as his authority, a member became sometimes so much heated as to launch into a flood of "real swearing," which brought the fists of the club upon his naked carcass as quick as hail.

These and other pastimes beguiled the time until, to my delight, the church chimes audibly tolled twelve. After this the noise gradually subsided, and it seemed as though everybody was going to sleep at last. I should have mentioned that during the story-telling and song-singing a few "casuals" had dropped in, but they were not *habitués*, and cuddled down with their rugs over their heads without a word to any one.

In a little while all was quiet, save for the flapping of the canvas curtain in the night breeze, the snoring, and the horrible, indescribable sound of impatient hands scratching skins that itch. There was another sound of very frequent occurrence, and that was the clanking of the tin pannikin against the water-pail. Whether it is in thenature of workhouse bread or skilley to provoke thirst is more than my limited experience entitles me to say, but it may be truthfully asserted that once at least in the course of five minutes might be heard a rustling of straw, pattering of feet, and then the noise of water dipping, and then was to be seen at the pail the figure of a man (sometimes stark naked) gulping down the icy water as he stood upon the icy stones.

And here I may remark that I can furnish no solution to this mystery of the shirt. I only know that some of my comrades were provided with a shirt, and that to some the luxury was denied. I may say this, however, that none of the little boys were allowed one.

Nearly one o'clock. Still quiet and no fresh arrival for an hour or more. Then suddenly a loud noise of hobnailed boots kicked at a wooden gate, and soon after a tramping of feet and a rapping at Daddy's door, which, it will be remembered, was only separated from our bedroom by an open paved court.

"Hallo!" cried Daddy.

"Here's some more of 'em for you,—ten of 'em!" answered the porter, whose voice I recognized at once.

"They'll have to find beds, then," Daddy grumbled, as he opened his door. "I don't believe there are four beds empty. They must sleep double, or something."

This was terrible news for me. Bad enough, in all conscience, was it to lie as I was lying; but the prospect of sharing my straw with some dirty scoundrel of the Kay breed was altogether unendurable. Perhaps, however, they were not dirty scoundrels, but peaceable and decent men, like those in the farther corner.

Alas for my hopes! In the space of five minutes in they came at the rent in the canvas,—great hulking ruffians, some with rugs and nothing else, and some with shirts and nothing else, and all madly swearing because, coming in after eleven o'clock, there was no "toke" for them. As soon as these wrathful men had advanced to the middle of the shed they made the discovery that there was an insufficient number of beds,—only three, indeed, for ten competitors.

"Where's the beds? D' ye hear, Daddy? You blessed, truth-telling old person, where's the beds?"

"You'll find 'em. Some of 'em is lying on two, or got 'em as pillows. You'll find 'em."

With a sudden rush our new friends plunged among the sleepers, trampling over them, cursing their eyes and limbs, dragging away their rugs; and if by chance they found some poor wretch who had been tempted to take two beds (or bags) instead of one, they coolly hauled him out and took possession. There was no denying them and no use in remonstrating. They evidently knew that they were at liberty to do just as they liked, and they took full advantage of the privilege.

One of them came up to me, and shouting, "I want that, you ——," snatched at my "birdseye" nightcap and carried it off. There was a bed close to mine which contained only one occupant, and into this one of the new-comers slipped without a word of warning, driving its lawful owner against the wall to make room. Then he sat up in bed for a moment, savagely venting his disappointment as to "toke," and declaring that never before in his life had he felt the need of it so much.This was my opportunity. Slipping my hand under my bed, I withdrew that judiciously hoarded piece of bread and respectfully offered it to him. He snapped at it with thanks.

By the time the churches were chiming two matters had once more adjusted themselves, and silence reigned, to be disturbed only by drinkers at the pail, or such as, otherwise prompted, stalked into the open yard. Kay, for one, visited it. I mention this unhappy young wretch particularly, because he went out without a single rag to his back. I looked out at the rent in the canvas, and saw the frosty moon shining on him. When he returned, and crept down between Punch and another, he muttered to himself, "Warm again! O my G-d! warm again!"

I hope, Mr. Editor, that you will not think me too prodigal of these reminiscences, and that your readers will understand that, if I write rather boldly, it is not done as a matter of taste. To me it seems quite worth while to relate with tolerable accuracy every particular of an adventure which you persuaded me ("ah! woful when!") to undertake for the public good.

Whether there is a rule which closes the casual wards after a certain hour I do not know; but before one o'clock our number was made up, the last-comer signalizing his appearance with a grotesque *pas seul.* His rug over his shoulders, he waltzed into the shed, waving his hands, and singing in an affected voice, as he sidled along,—

"I like to be a swell, a-roaming down Pall-Mall,

Or anywhere, I don't much care, so I can be a swell,"—

a couplet which had an intensely comical effect. This gentleman had just come from a pantomime (where he had learnt his song, probably). Too poor to pay for a lodging, he could only muster means for a seat in the gallery of "the Vic," where he was well entertained, judging from the flattering manner in which he spoke of the clown. The columbine was less fortunate in his opinion. "She's werry dickey!—ain't got what I call 'move' about her." However, the wretched young woman was respited now from the scourge of his criticism; for the critic and his listeners were fast asleep; and yet I doubt whether any one of the company slept very soundly. Every moment some one shifted uneasily; and as the night wore on the silence was more and more irritated by the sound of coughing. This was one of the most distressing things in the whole adventure. The conversation was horrible, the tales that were told more horrible still, and worse than either (though not by any means the most infamous things to be heard,—I dare not even hint at them) was that song, with its bestial chorus shouted from a dozen throats; but at any rate they kept the blood warm with constant hot flushes of anger; while as for the coughing, to lie on the flagstones in what was nothing better than an open shed, and listen to that, hour after hour, chilled one's very heart with pity. Every variety of cough that ever I heard was to be heard there: the hollow cough; the short cough; the hysterical cough; the bark that comes at regular intervals, like the quarter-chime of a clock, as if to mark off the progress of decay; coughing from vast hollow chests, coughing from little narrow ones,—now one, now another, now two or three together,and then a minute's interval of silence in which to think of it all and wonder who would begin next. One of the young reprobates above me coughed so grotesquely, like the chopping of wood, that I named him in my mind the Woodcutter. Now and then I found myself coughing too, which may have added just a little to the poignant distress these awfully constant and various sounds occasioned me. They were good in one way; they made one forget what wretches they were who, to all appearances, were so rapidly "chopping" their way to a pauper's graveyard. I did not care about the more matured ruffians so much; but though the youngest, the boys like Kay, were unquestionably among the most infamous of my comrades, to hear what cold and hunger and vice had done for them at fifteen was almost enough to make a man cry; and there were boys there even younger than these.

At half past two, every one being asleep, or at least lying still, Daddy came in and counted us,—one, two, three, four, and so on, in a whisper. Then, finding the pail empty (it was nearly full at half past nine, when I entered), he considerately went and refilled it, and even took much trouble in searching for the tin pot which served as a drinking-cup, and which the last-comer had playfully thrown to the farther end of the shed. I ought to have mentioned that the pail stood close to my head; so that I had peculiar opportunities of study as one after another of my comrades came to the fountain to drink; just as the brutes do in those books of African travel. The pail refilled, Daddy returned, and was seen no more till morning.

It still wanted four hours and a half to seven o'clock,—thehour of rising,—and never before in my life did time appear to creep so slowly. I could hear the chimes of a parish church and of the Parliament Houses, as well as those of a wretched, tinkling Dutch clock somewhere on the premises. The parish church was the first to announce the hour (an act of kindness I feel bound to acknowledge), Westminster came next, the lazy Dutchman declining his consent to the time o' day till fully sixty seconds afterwards. And I declare I thought that difference of sixty seconds an injury,—if the officers of the house took their time from the Dutchman. It may seem a trifle, but a minute is something when a man is lying on a cold flagstone, and the wind of a winter night is blowing in your hair. Three o'clock, four o'clock struck, and still there was nothing to beguile the time, but observation, under the one flaring gaslight, of the little heaps of outcast humanity strewn about the floor; and after a while, I find, one may even become accustomed to the sight of one's fellow-creatures lying around you like covered corpses in a railway shed. For most of the company were now bundled under the rugs in the ghastly way I have already described,—though here and there a cropped head appeared, surmounted by a billy-cock like my own or by a greasy cloth cap. Five o'clock, six o'clock chimed, and then I had news—most welcome—of the world without, and of the real beginning of day. Half a dozen factory bells announced that it was time for workingmen to go to labor; but my companions were not workingmen, and so snored on. Out through the gap in the canvas the stars were still to be seen shining on the black sky; but that did not alter thefact that it was six o'clock in the morning. I snapped my fingers at the Dutchman, with his sixty seconds slow, for in another hour I fondly hoped to be relieved from duty. A little while, and doors were heard to open and shut; yet a little while, and the voice of Daddy was audible in conversation with another early bird; and then I distinctly caught the word "bundles." Blessed sound! I longed for my bundle,—for my pleasing brown coat, for the warm—if unsightly—"jersey," which I adopted as a judicious substitute for a waistcoat,—for my corduroys and liberty.

"Clang!" went the workhouse clock. "Now, then, wake 'em up!" cried Daddy. I was already up,—sitting up, that is,—being anxious to witness the resurrection of the ghastly figures rolled in their rugs. But nobody but myself rose at the summons. They knew what it meant well enough, and in sleepy voices cursed the bell, and wished it in several dreadful places; but they did not move until there came in at the hole in the canvas two of the pauper inhabitants of the house, bearing bundles. "Thirty-two," "Twenty-eight!" they bawled, but not *my* number, which was thirty-four. Neither thirty-two nor twenty-eight, however, seemed eager to accept his good fortune in being first called. They were called upon three several times before they would answer; and then they replied with a savage, "Chuck it here, can't you!" "Not before you chucks over your shirt and ticket," the bundle-holder answered; whereon "twenty-eight" sat up, and, divesting himself of his borrowed shirt, flung it with his wooden ticket; and his bundle was flung back in return.

It was some time before bundle No. 34 turned up, so that I had fair opportunity to observe my neighbors. The decent men slipped into their rags as soon as they got them, but the blackguards were in no hurry. Some indulged in a morning pipe to prepare themselves for the fatigue of dressing, while others, loosening their bundles as they squatted naked, commenced an investigation for certain little animals which shall be nameless.

At last my turn came, and, "chucking over" my shirt and ticket, I quickly attired myself in clothes which, ragged as they were, were cleaner than they looked. In less than two minutes I was out of the shed, and in the yard; where a few of the more decent poor fellows were crowding round a pail of water, and scrambling after something that might pass for a "wash,"— finding their own soap, as far as I could observe, and drying their faces on any bit of rag they might happen to have about them, or upon the canvas curtain of the shed.

By this time it was about half past seven, and the majority of the casuals were up and dressed. I observed, however, that none of the younger boys were as yet up, and it presently appeared that there existed some rule against their dressing in the shed; for Daddy came out of the bath-room, where the bundles were deposited, and called out, "Now four boys!" and instantly four poor little wretches, some with their rugs trailing about their shoulders and some quite bare, came shivering over the stones and across the bleak yard, and were admitted to the bath-room to dress. "Now, four more boys," cried Daddy; and so on.

When all were up and dressed, the boys carried thebed-rugs into Daddy's room, and the pauper inmates made a heap of the "beds," stacking them against the wall. As before mentioned, the shed served the treble purpose of bedchamber, work-room, and breakfast-room; it was impossible to get fairly at the cranks and set them going until the bedding was stowed away.

Breakfast before work, however; but it was a weary while to some of us before it made its appearance. For my own part, I had little appetite, but about me were a dozen poor wretches who obviously had a very great one. They had come in overnight too late for bread, and perhaps may not have broken fast since the morning of the previous day. The decent ones suffered most. The blackguard majority were quite cheerful, smoking, swearing, and playing their pretty horse play, the prime end of which was pain or discomfiture for somebody else. One casual there was with only one leg. When he came in overnight he wore a black hat, which added a certain look of respectability to a worn suit of black. All together his clothes had been delivered up to him by Daddy; but now he was seen hopping disconsolately about the place on his crutch, for the hat was missing. He was a timid man, with a mild voice; and whenever he asked some ruffian "whether he had seen such a thing as a black hat," and got his answer, he invariably said, "Thank you," which was regarded as very amusing. At last one sidled up to him with a grin, and showing about three square inches of some fluffy substance, said, "Is this anything like wot you're lost, guv'ner?" The cripple inspected it. "That's the rim of it!" he said. "What a shame!" and hobbled off with tears in his eyes.

Full three quarters of an hour of loitering and shivering, and then came the taskmaster,—a soldierly looking man over six feet high, with quick, gray eyes, in which "No trifling" appeared as distinctly as a notice against trespassing on a wayside board. He came in among us, and the gray eyes made out our number in a moment. "Out into the yard, all of you!" he cried; and we went out in a mob. There we shivered for some twenty minutes longer, and then a baker's man appeared with a great wooden tray piled up with just such slices of bread as we had received overnight. The tray was consigned to an able-bodied casual who took his place with the taskmaster at the shed door, and then in single file we re-entered the shed, each man and boy receiving a slice as he passed in. Pitying, as I suppose, my unaccustomed look, Mr. Taskmaster gave me a slice and a large piece over.

The bread devoured, a clamor for "skilley" began. The rumor had got abroad that this morning, and on all future mornings, there would be skilley at breakfast, and "Skilley! skilley!" resounded through the shed. No one had hinted that it was not forthcoming, but skilley seems to be thought an extraordinary concession, and after waiting only a few minutes for it they attacked the taskmaster in the fiercest manner. They called him thief, sneak, and "crawler." Little boys blackguarded him in gutter language, and looking him in the face, consigned him to hell without flinching. He never uttered a word in reply, or showed a sign of impatience; and whenever he was obliged to speak it was quite without temper.

There was a loud "hooray!" when the longed-for skilley appeared in two pails, in one of which floated asmall tin saucepan, with a stick thrust into its handle, by way of a ladle. Yellow pint basins were provided for our use, and large iron spoons. "Range round the walls!" the taskmaster shouted. We obeyed with the utmost alacrity; and then what I should judge to be about three fourths of a pint of gruel was handed to each of us as we stood. I was glad to get mine, because the basin that contained it was warm and my hands were numb with cold. I tasted a spoonful, as in duty bound, and wondered more than ever at the esteem in which it was held by my *confrères*. It was a weak decoction of oatmeal and water, bitter, and without even a pinch of salt to flavor it,—that I could discover. But it was hot; and on that account, perhaps, was so highly relished that I had no difficulty in persuading one of the decent men to accept my share.

It was now past eight o'clock, and, as I knew that a certain quantity of labor had to be performed by each man before he was allowed to go his way, I was anxious to begin. The labor was to be "crank" labor. The "cranks" are a series of iron bars extending across the width of the shed, penetrating through the wall, and working a flour-mill on the other side. Turning the "crank" is like turning a windlass. The task is not a severe one. Four measures of corn (bushels they were called, but that is doubtful) have to be ground every morning by the night's batch of casuals. Close up by the ceiling hangs a bell connected with the machinery; and as each measure is ground the bell rings, so that the grinders may know how they are going on. But the grinders are as lazy as obscene. We were no sooner setto work than the taskmaster left us to our own sweet will, with nothing to restrain its exercise but an occasional visit from the miller, a weakly expostulating man. Once or twice he came in and said mildly, "Now then, my men, why don't you stick to it?" and so went out again.

The result of this laxity of overseeing would have disgusted me at any time, and was intensely disgusting then. At least one half the gang kept their hands from the crank whenever the miller was absent, and betook themselves to their private amusements and pursuits. Some sprawled upon the beds and smoked; some engaged themselves and their friends in tailoring; and one turned hair-cutter for the benefit of a gentleman, who, unlike Kay, had not just come out of prison. There were three tailors; two of them on the beds mending their coats, and the other operating on a recumbent friend in the rearward part of his clothing. Where the needles came from I do not know; but for thread they used a strand of the oakum (evidently easy to deal with) which the boys were picking in the corners. Other loungers strolled about with their hands in their pockets, discussing the topics of the day, and playing practical jokes on the industrious few; a favorite joke being to take a bit of rag, anoint it with grease from the crank axles, and clap it unexpectedly over somebody's eye.

The consequence of all this was that the cranks went round at a very slow rate, and now and then stopped altogether. Then the miller came in; the loungers rose from their couches, the tailors ceased stitching, the smokers dropped their pipes, and every fellow was at his post.The cranks spun round furiously again, the miller's expostulation being drowned amid a shout of, "Slap bang, here we are again!" or this extemporized chorus:—

"We'll hang up the miller on a sour-apple tree,

We'll hang up the miller on a sour-apple tree,

We'll hang up the miller on a sour-apple tree,

And then go grinding on.

Glory, glory, Hallelujah," etc.

By such ditties the ruffians enlivened their short spell of work. Short indeed! The miller departed, and within a minute afterward beds were reoccupied, pipes lit, and tailoring resumed. So the game continued,—the honest fellows sweating at the cranks, and anxious to get the work done and go out to look for more profitable labor, and the paupers by profession taking matters quite easy. I am convinced that had the work been properly superintended the four measures of corn might have been ground in the space of an hour and a half. As it was, when the little bell had tinkled for the fourth time, and the yard-gate was opened, and we were free to depart, the clock had struck eleven.

I had seen the show; gladly I escaped into the open streets. The sun shone brightly on my ragged, disreputable figure, and showed its squalor with startling distinctness; but within all was rejoicing. A few yards, and then I was blessed with the sight of that same vehicle, waiting for me in the spot where I had parted from it fourteen weary hours before. Did you observe, Mr. Editor, with what alacrity I jumped in? I have a vividrecollection of you, sir, sitting there with an easy patience, lounging through your *Times*, and oh! so detestably clean to look at! But though I resented your collar, I was grateful for the sight of a familiar face, and for that draught of sherry which you considerately brought for me, a welcome refreshment after so many weary, waking hours of fasting.

And now I have come to the end I remember many little incidents which until this moment had escaped me. I ought to have told you of two quiet elderly gentlemen who, amid all the blackguardism that went on around, held a discussion on the merits of the English language,—one of the disputants showing an especial admiration for the word "kindle,"—"fine old Saxon word as ever was coined." Then there were some childish games of "first and last letters," to vary such entertainments as that of the Swearing Club. I should also have mentioned that, on the dissolution of the Swearing Club, a game at "dumb motions" was started, which presently led to some talk concerning deaf and dumb people, and their method of conversing with each other by means of finger-signs; as well as to a little story that sounded strangely enough coming from the mouth of the most efficient member of the club. A good memory for details enables me to repeat this story almost, if not quite, exactly. "They are a rummy lot, them deaf and dumb," said the story-teller. "I was at the workhouse at Stepney when I was a young 'un, don't you know; and when I got a holiday I used to go and see my old woman as lived in the Borough. Well, one day a woman as was in the house ses to me, ses she, 'Don't you go past the Deaf andDumb School as you goes home?' So I ses, 'Yes.' So ses she, 'Would you mind callin' there and takin' a message to my little gal as is in there deaf and dumb?' So I ses, 'No.' Well, I goes, and they lets me in, and I tells the message, and they shows me the kid what it was for. Pooty little gal! So they tells her the message, and then she begins making orts and crosses like on her hands. 'What's she a doin' that for?' I ses. 'She's a talkin' to you,' ses they. 'O,' I ses, 'what's she talkin' about?' 'She says you're a good boy for comin' and tellin' her about her mother, and she loves you.' Blessed if I could help laughin'! So I ses, 'There ain't no call for her to say that.' Pooty little kid she was! I stayed there a goodish bit, and walked about the garden with her, and what d'ye think? Presently she takes a fancy for some of my jacket buttons,—brass uns they was, with the name of the 'house' on 'em,— and I cuts four on 'em off and gives her. Well, when I gave her them blow me if she didn't want one of the brass buckles off my shoes. Well, you mightn't think it, but I gave her that too." "Didn't yer get into a row when you got back?" some listener asked. "Rather! Got kep without dinner and walloped as well, as I wouldn't tell what I'd done with 'em. Then they was goin' to wallop me again, so I thought I'd cheek it out; so I up and told the master all about it." "And got it wuss?" "No, I didn't. The master give me new buttons and a buckle without saying another word, and my dinner along with my supper as well."

THE OUTCASTS OF POKER FLAT.

BY BRET HARTE.

As Mr. John Oakhurst, gambler, stepped into the main street of Poker Flat, on the morning of the 23d of November, 1850, he was conscious of a change in its moral atmosphere since the preceding night. Two or three men, conversing earnestly together, ceased as he approached, and exchanged significant glances. There was a Sabbath lull in the air, which, in a settlement unused to Sabbath influences, looked ominous.

Mr. Oakhurst's calm, handsome face betrayed small concern in these indications. Whether he was conscious of any predisposing cause, was another question. "I reckon they're after somebody," he reflected; "likely it's me." He returned to his pocket the handkerchief with which he had been whipping away the red dust of Poker Flat from his neat boots, and quietly discharged his mind of any further conjecture.

In point of fact, Poker Flat was "after somebody." It had lately suffered the loss of several thousand dollars,two valuable horses, and a prominent citizen. It was experiencing a spasm of virtuous reaction, quite as lawless and ungovernable as any of the acts that had provoked it. A secret committee had determined to rid the town of all improper persons. This was done permanently in regard of two men who were then hanging from the boughs of a sycamore in the gulch, and temporarily in the banishment of certain other objectionable characters. I regret to say that some of these were ladies. It is but due to the sex, however, to state that their impropriety was professional, and it was only in such easily established standards of evil that Poker Flat ventured to sit in judgment.

Mr. Oakhurst was right in supposing that he was included in this category. A few of the committee had urged hanging him as a possible example, and a sure method of reimbursing themselves from his pockets of the sums he had won from them. "It's agin justice," said Jim Wheeler, "to let this yer young man from Roaring Camp—an entire stranger—carry away our money." But a crude sentiment of equity, residing in the breasts of those who had been fortunate enough to win from Mr. Oakhurst, overruled this narrower local prejudice.

Mr. Oakhurst received his sentence with philosophic calmness, none the less coolly that he was aware of the hesitation of his judges. He was too much of a gambler not to accept Fate.

With him life was at best an uncertain game, and he recognized the usual percentage in favor of the dealer. A body of armed men accompanied the deported wickednessof Poker Flat to the outskirts of the settlement. Besides Mr. Oakhurst, who was known to be a coolly desperate man, and for whose intimidation the armed escort was intended, the expatriated party consisted of a young woman familiarly known as "The Duchess"; another, who had won the title of "Mother Shipton"; and "Uncle Billy," a suspected sluice-robber and confirmed drunkard. The cavalcade provoked no comments from the spectators, nor was any word uttered by the escort. Only, when the gulch which marked the uttermost limit of Poker Flat was reached, the leader spoke briefly and to the point. The exiles were forbidden to return, at the peril of their lives. As the escort disappeared, their pent-up feelings found vent in a few hysterical tears from the Duchess, some bad language from Mother Shipton, and a Parthian volley of expletives from Uncle Billy. The philosophic Oakhurst alone remained silent. He listened calmly to Mother Shipton's desire to cut somebody's heart out, to the repeated statements of the Duchess that she would die in the road, and to the alarming oaths that seemed to be bumped out of Uncle Billy as he rode forward. With the easy good-humor characteristic of his class, he insisted upon exchanging his own riding-horse, "Five Spot," for the sorry mule which the Duchess rode. But even this act did not draw the party into any closer sympathy. The young woman readjusted her somewhat draggled plumes with a feeble, faded coquetry; Mother Shipton eyed the possessor of "Five Spot" with malevolence; and Uncle Billy included the whole party in one sweeping anathema.

The road to Sandy Bar—a camp that, not having as yet experienced the regenerating influences of Poker Flat, consequently seemed to offer some invitation to the emigrants—lay over a steep mountain range. It was distant a day's severe travel. In that advanced season, the party soon passed out of the moist, temperate regions of the foot-hills, into the dry, cold, bracing air of the Sierras. The trail was narrow and difficult. At noon the Duchess, rolling out of her saddle upon the ground, declared her intention of going no farther, and the party halted.

The spot was singularly wild and impressive. A wooded amphitheatre, surrounded on three sides by precipitous cliffs of naked granite, sloped gently toward the crest of another precipice that overlooked the valley. It was, undoubtedly, the most suitable spot for a camp, had camping been advisable. But Mr. Oakhurst knew that scarcely half the journey to Sandy Bar was accomplished, and the party were not equipped or provisioned for delay. This fact he pointed out to his companions curtly, with a philosophic commentary on the folly of "throwing up their hands before the game was played out." But they were furnished with liquor, which in this emergency stood them in place of food, fuel, rest, and prescience. In spite of his remonstrances, it was not long before they were more or less under its influence. Uncle Billy passed rapidly from a bellicose state into one of stupor, the Duchess became maudlin, and Mother Shipton snored. Mr. Oakhurst alone remained erect, leaning against a rock, calmly surveying them.

Mr. Oakhurst did not drink. It interfered with a professionwhich required coolness, impassiveness, and presence of mind, and, in his own language, he "couldn't afford it." As he gazed at his recumbent fellow-exiles, the loneliness begotten of his pariah-trade, his habits of life, his very vices, for the first time seriously oppressed him. He bestirred himself in dusting his black clothes, washing his hands and face, and other acts characteristic of his studiously neat habits, and for a moment forgot his annoyance. The thought of deserting his weaker and more pitiable companions never perhaps occurred to him. Yet he could not help feeling the want of that excitement which, singularly enough, was most conducive to that calm equanimity for which he was notorious. He looked at the gloomy walls that rose a thousand feet sheer above the circling pines around him; at the sky, ominously clouded; at the valley below, already deepening into shadow. And, doing so, suddenly he heard his own name called.

A horseman slowly ascended the trail. In the fresh, open face of the new-comer Mr. Oakhurst recognized Tom Simson, otherwise known as "The Innocent" of Sandy Bar. He had met him some months before over a "little game," and had, with perfect equanimity, won the entire fortune— amounting to some forty dollars—of that guileless youth. After the game was finished, Mr. Oakhurst drew the youthful speculator behind the door and thus addressed him: "Tommy, you're a good little man, but you can't gamble worth a cent. Don't try it over again." He then handed him his money back, pushed him gently from the room, and so made a devoted slave of Tom Simson.

There was a remembrance of this in his boyish and enthusiastic greeting of Mr. Oakhurst. He had started, he said, to go to Poker Flat to seek his fortune. "Alone?" No, not exactly alone; in fact (a giggle), he had run away with Piney Woods. Didn't Mr. Oakhurst remember Piney? She that used to wait on the table at the Temperance House? They had been engaged a long time, but old Jake Woods had objected, and so they had run away, and were going to Poker Flat to be married, and here they were. And they were tired out, and how lucky it was they had found a place to camp and company. All this the Innocent delivered rapidly, while Piney, a stout, comely damsel of fifteen, emerged from behind the pine-tree, where she had been blushing unseen, and rode to the side of her lover.

Mr. Oakhurst seldom troubled himself with sentiment, still less with propriety; but he had a vague idea that the situation was not fortunate. He retained, however, his presence of mind sufficiently to kick Uncle Billy, who was about to say something, and Uncle Billy was sober enough to recognize in Mr. Oakhurst's kick a superior power that would not bear trifling. He then endeavored to dissuade Tom Simson from delaying further, but in vain. He even pointed out the fact that there was no provision, nor means for making a camp. But, unluckily, the Innocent met this objection by assuring the party that he was provided with an extra mule loaded with provisions, and by the discovery of a rude attempt at a log-house near the trail. "Piney can stay with Mrs. Oakhurst," said the Innocent, pointing to the Duchess, "and I can shift for myself."

Nothing but Mr. Oakhurst's admonishing foot saved Uncle Billy from bursting into a roar of laughter. As it was, he felt compelled to retire up the cañon until he could recover his gravity. There he confided the joke to the tall pine-trees, with many slaps of his leg, contortions of his face, and the usual profanity. But when he returned to the party, he found them seated by a fire—for the air had grown strangely chill, and the sky overcast—in apparently amicable conversation. Piney was actually talking in an impulsive, girlish fashion to the Duchess, who was listening with an interest and animation she had not shown for many days. The Innocent was holding forth, apparently with equal effect, to Mr. Oakhurst and Mother Shipton, who was actually relaxing into amiability.

"Is this yer a d—d picnic?" said Uncle Billy, with inward scorn, as he surveyed the sylvan group, the glancing firelight, and the tethered animals in the foreground. Suddenly an idea mingled with the alcoholic fumes that disturbed his brain. It was apparently of a jocular nature, for he felt impelled to slap his leg again, and cram his fist into his mouth.

As the shadows crept slowly up the mountain, a slight breeze rocked the tops of the pine-trees, and moaned through their long and gloomy aisles. The ruined cabin, patched and covered with pine boughs, was set apart for the ladies. As the lovers parted, they unaffectedly exchanged a kiss, so honest and sincere that it might have been heard above the swaying pines. The frail Duchess and the malevolent Mother Shipton were probably too stunned to remark upon this last evidence of simplicity,and so turned without a word to the hut. The fire was replenished, the men lay down before the door, and in a few minutes were asleep.

Mr. Oakhurst was a light sleeper. Toward morning he awoke benumbed and cold. As he stirred the dying fire, the wind, which was now blowing strongly, brought to his cheek that which caused the blood to leave it,— snow!

He started to his feet with the intention of awakening the sleepers, for there was no time to lose. But turning to where Uncle Billy had been lying, he found him gone. A suspicion leaped to his brain, and a curse to his lips. He ran to the spot where the mules had been tethered; they were no longer there. The tracks were already rapidly disappearing in the snow.

The momentary excitement brought Mr. Oakhurst back to the fire with his usual calm. He did not waken the sleepers. The Innocent slumbered peacefully, with a smile on his good-humored, freckled face; the virgin Piney slept beside her frailer sisters as sweetly as though attended by celestial guardians; and Mr. Oakhurst, drawing his blanket over his shoulders, stroked his mustaches and waited for the dawn. It came slowly in a whirling mist of snow-flakes, that dazzled and confused the eye. What could be seen of the landscape appeared magically changed. He looked over the valley, and summed up the present and future in two words,—"Snowed in!"

A careful inventory of the provisions, which, fortunately for the party, had been stored within the hut, and so escaped the felonious fingers of Uncle Billy, disclosedthe fact that with care and prudence they might last ten days longer. "That is," said Mr. Oakhurst, *sotto voce* to the Innocent, "if you're willing to board us. If you ain't—and perhaps you'd better not—we can wait till Uncle Billy gets back with provisions." For some occult reason, Mr. Oakhurst could not bring himself to disclose Uncle Billy's rascality, and so offered the hypothesis that he had wandered from the camp and had accidentally stampeded the animals. He dropped a warning to the Duchess and Mother Shipton, who of course knew the facts of their associate's defection. "They'll find out the truth about us *all* when they find out anything," he added, significantly, "and there's no good frightening them now."

Tom Simson not only put all his worldly store at the disposal of Mr. Oakhurst, but seemed to enjoy the prospect of their enforced seclusion. "We'll have a good camp for a week, and then the snow'll melt, and we'll all go back together."

The cheerful gayety of the young man, and Mr. Oakhurst's calm, infected the others. The Innocent, with the aid of pine boughs, extemporized a thatch for the roofless cabin, and the Duchess directed Piney in the rearrangement of the interior, with a taste and tact that opened the blue eyes of that provincial maiden to their fullest extent.

"I reckon now you're used to fine things at Poker Flat," said Piney.

The Duchess turned away sharply, to conceal something that reddened her cheek through its professional tint, and Mother Shipton requested Piney not to "chatter." But when Mr. Oakhurst returned from a weary search for the trail, he heard the sound of happy laughter echoed from the rocks. He stopped in some alarm, and his thoughts first naturally reverted to the whiskey, which he had prudently *cachéd*. "And yet it don't somehow sound like whiskey," said the gambler. It was not until he caught sight of the blazing fire through the still blinding storm, and the group around it, that he settled to the conviction that it was "square fun."

Whether Mr. Oakhurst had *cachéd* his cards with the whiskey, as something debarred the free access of the community, I cannot say. It was certain that, in Mother Shipton's words, he "didn't say cards once" during that evening. Haply the time was beguiled by an accordion, produced somewhat ostentatiously by Tom Simson from his pack. Notwithstanding some difficulties attending the manipulation of this instrument, Piney Woods managed to pluck several reluctant melodies from its keys, to an accompaniment by the Innocent on a pair of bone castinets. But the crowning festivity of the evening was reached in a rude camp-meeting hymn, which the lovers, joining hands, sang with great earnestness and vociferation. I fear that a certain defiant tone and covenanter's swing to its chorus, rather than any devotional quality, caused it speedily to infect the others, who at last joined in the refrain:—

"I'm proud to live in the service of the Lord,

And I'm bound to die in his army."

The pines rocked, the storm eddied and whirled above the miserable group, and the flames of their altar leaped heavenward, as if in token of the vow.

At midnight the storm abated, the rolling clouds parted, and the stars glittered keenly above the sleeping camp. Mr. Oakhurst, whose professional habits had enabled him to live on the smallest possible amount of sleep, in dividing the watch with Tom Simson, somehow managed to take upon himself the greater part of that duty. He excused himself to the Innocent by saying that he had "often been a week without sleep."

"Doing what?" asked Tom. "Poker!" replied Oakhurst, sententiously; "when a man gets a streak of luck,—nigger-luck,—he don't get tired. The luck gives in first. Luck," continued the gambler, reflectively, "is a mighty queer thing. All you know about it for certain is that it's bound to change. And it's finding out when it's going to change that makes you. We've had a streak of bad luck since we left Poker Flat; you come along, and slap you get into it too. If you can hold your cards right along, you're all right. For," added the gambler, with cheerful irrelevance,—

"I'm proud to live in the service of the Lord,

And I'm bound to die in his army."

The third day came, and the sun, looking through the white-curtained valley, saw the outcasts divide their slowly decreasing store of provisions for the morning meal. It was one of the peculiarities of that mountain climate that its rays diffused a kindly warmth over the wintry landscape, as if in regretful commiseration of the past. But it revealed drift on drift of snow piled high around the hut,—a hopeless, uncharted, trackless sea of white, lying below the rocky shores to which the castaways still clung. Through the marvellously clear air the smoke of the pastoral village of Poker Flat rose miles away. Mother Shipton saw it, and from a remote pinnacle of her rocky fastness hurled in that direction a final malediction. It was her last vituperative attempt, and perhaps for that reason was invested with a certain degree of sublimity. It did her good, she privately informed the Duchess. "Just you go out there and cuss, and see." She then set herself to the task of amusing "the child," as she and the Duchess were pleased to call Piney. Piney was no chicken, but it was a soothing and original theory of the pair thus to account for the fact that she didn't swear and wasn't improper.

When night crept up again through the gorges, the reedy notes of the accordion rose and fell in fitful spasms and long-drawn gasps by the flickering camp-fire. But music failed to fill entirely the aching void left by insufficient food, and a new diversion was proposed by Piney,—story-telling. Neither Mr. Oakhurst nor his female companions caring to relate their personal experiences, this plan would have failed too, but for the Innocent. Some months before he had chanced upon a stray copy of Mr. Pope's ingenious translation of the Iliad. He now proposed to narrate the principal incidents of that poem—having thoroughly mastered the argument and fairly forgotten the words—in the current vernacular of Sandy Bar. And so for the rest of that night the Homeric demigods again walked the earth. Trojan bully and wily Greek wrestled in the winds, and the great pines in the cañon seemed to bow to the wrath ofthe son of Peleus. Mr. Oakhurst listened with quiet satisfaction. Most especially was he interested in the fate of "Ash-heels," as the Innocent persisted in denominating the "swift-footed Achilles."

So with small food and much of Homer and the accordion, a week passed over the heads of the outcasts. The sun again forsook them, and again from leaden skies the snow-flakes were sifted over the land. Day by day closer around them drew the snowy circle, until at last they looked from their prison over drifted walls of dazzling white, that towered twenty feet above their heads. It became more and more difficult to replenish their fires, even from the fallen trees beside them, now half hidden in the drifts. And yet no one complained. The lovers turned from the dreary prospect and looked into each other's eyes, and were happy. Mr. Oakhurst settled himself coolly to the losing game before him. The Duchess, more cheerful than she had been, assumed the care of Piney. Only Mother Shipton—once the strongest of the party—seemed to sicken and fade. At midnight on the tenth day she called Oakhurst to her side.

"I'm going," she said, in a voice of querulous weakness, "but don't say anything about it. Don't waken the kids. Take the bundle from under my head, and open it." Mr. Oakhurst did so. It contained Mother Shipton's rations for the last week, untouched. "Give 'em to the child," she said, pointing to the sleeping Piney.

"You've starved yourself," said the gambler.

"That's what they call it," said the woman, querulously, as she lay down again, and, turning her face to the wall, passed quietly away.

The accordion and the bones were put aside that day, and Homer was forgotten. When the body of Mother Shipton had been committed to the snow, Mr. Oakhurst took the Innocent aside, and showed him a pair of snow-shoes, which he had fashioned from the old pack-saddle.

"There's one chance in a hundred to save her yet," he said, pointing to Piney; "but it's there," he added, pointing toward Poker Flat. "If you can reach there in two days, she's safe."

"And you?" asked Tom Simson.

"I'll stay here," was the curt reply.

The lovers parted with a long embrace. "You are not going, too?" said the Duchess, as she saw Mr. Oakhurst apparently waiting to accompany him.

"As far as the cañon," he replied. He turned suddenly, and kissed the Duchess, leaving her pallid face aflame, and her trembling limbs rigid with amazement.

Night came, but not Mr. Oakhurst. It brought the storm again and the whirling snow. Then the Duchess, feeding the fire, found that some one had quietly piled beside the hut enough fuel to last a few days longer. The tears rose to her eyes, but she hid them from Piney.

The women slept but little. In the morning, looking into each other's faces, they read their fate. Neither spoke; but Piney, accepting the position of the stronger, drew near and placed her arm around the Duchess's waist. They kept this attitude for the rest of the day. That night the storm reached its greatest fury, and rending asunder the protecting pines, invaded the very hut.

Toward morning they found themselves unable to feed the fire, which gradually died away. As the embers slowly blackened, the Duchess crept closer to Piney, and broke the silence of many hours: "Piney, can you pray?"

"No, dear," said Piney, simply. The Duchess, without knowing exactly why, felt relieved, and, putting her head upon Piney's shoulder, spoke no more. And so reclining, the younger and purer pillowing the head of her soiled sister upon her virgin breast, they fell asleep.

The wind lulled as if it feared to waken them. Feathery drifts of snow, shaken from the long pine-boughs, flew like white-winged birds, and settled about them as they slept. The moon through the rifted clouds looked down upon what had been the camp. But all human stain, all trace of earthly travail, was hidden beneath the spotless mantle mercifully flung from above.

They slept all that day and the next; nor did they waken when voices and footsteps broke the silence of the camp. And when pitying fingers brushed the snow from their wan faces, you could scarcely have told from the equal peace that dwelt upon them, which was she that had sinned. Even the law of Poker Flat recognized this, and turned away, leaving them still locked in each other's arms.

But at the head of the gulch, on one of the largest pine-trees, they found the deuce of clubs pinned to the bark with a bowie-knife. It bore the following, written in pencil, in a firm hand:—

BENEATH THIS TREE
LIES THE BODY
OF
JOHN OAKHURST,
WHO STRUCK A STREAK OF BAD LUCK
ON THE 23D OF NOVEMBER, 1850,
AND
HANDED IN HIS CHECKS
ON THE 7TH DECEMBER, 1850.

And pulseless and cold, with a Derringer by his side and a bullet in his heart, though still calm as in life, beneath the snow lay he who was at once the strongest and yet the weakest of the outcasts of Poker Flat.

THE MAN WITHOUT A COUNTRY.

BY EDWARD EVERETT HALE.

I suppose that very few casual readers of the New York Herald of August 13th observed, in an obscure corner, among the "Deaths," the announcement,—

> "NOLAN. Died, on board U.S. Corvette Levant, Lat. 2° 11'
> S., Long. 131° W., on the 11th of May, PHILIP NOLAN."

I happened to observe it, because I was stranded at the old Mission-House in Mackinaw, waiting for a Lake Superior steamer which did not choose to come, and I was devouring to the very stubble all the current literature I could get hold of, even down to the deaths and marriages in the Herald. My memory for names and people is good, and the reader will see, as he goes on, that I had reason enough to remember Philip Nolan. There are hundreds of readers who would have paused at that announcement, if the officer of the Levant who reported it had chosen to make it thus:—"Died, May 11th, THE MAN WITHOUT A COUNTRY." For it was as "The Man without a Country" that poor Philip Nolanhad generally been known by the officers who had him in charge during some fifty years, as, indeed, by all the men who sailed under them. I dare say there is many a man who has taken wine with him once a fortnight, in a three years' cruise, who never knew that his name was "Nolan," or whether the poor wretch had any name at all.

There can now be no possible harm in telling this poor creature's story. Reason enough there has been till now, ever since Madison's administration went out in 1817, for very strict secrecy, the secrecy of honor itself, among the gentlemen of the navy who have had Nolan in successive charge. And certainly it speaks well for the *esprit de corps* of the profession and the personal honor of its members, that to the press this man's story has been wholly unknown,—and, I think, to the country at large also. I have reason to think, from some investigations I made in the Naval Archives when I was attached to the Bureau of Construction, that every official report relating to him was burned when Ross burned the public buildings at Washington. One of the Tuckers, or possibly one of the Watsons, had Nolan in charge at the end of the war; and when, on returning from his cruise, he reported at Washington to one of the Crowninshields,—who was in the Navy Department when he came home,—he found that the Department ignored the whole business. Whether they really knew nothing about it, or whether it was a "*Non mi ricordo*," determined on as a piece of policy, I do not know. But this I do know, that since 1817, and possibly before, no naval officer has mentioned Nolan in his report of a cruise.

But, as I say, there is no need for secrecy any longer. And now the poor creature is dead, it seems to me worth while to tell a little of his story, by way of showing young Americans of to-day what it is to be a man without a country.

Philip Nolan was as fine a young officer as there was in the "Legion of the West," as the Western division of our army was then called. When Aaron Burr made his first dashing expedition down to New Orleans in 1805, at Fort Massac, or somewhere above on the river, he met, as the Devil would have it, this gay, dashing, bright young fellow, at some dinner-party, I think. Burr marked him, talked to him, walked with him, took him a day or two's voyage in his flat-boat, and, in short, fascinated him. For the next year barrack-life was very tame to poor Nolan. He occasionally availed himself of the permission the great man had given him to write to him. Long, high-worded, stilted letters the poor boy wrote and rewrote and copied. But never a line did he have in reply from the gay deceiver. The other boys in the garrison sneered at him, because he sacrificed in this unrequited affection for a politician the time which they devoted to Monongahela, sledge, and high-low-jack. Bourbon, euchre, and poker were still unknown. But one day Nolan had his revenge. This time Burr came down the river, not as an attorney seeking a place for his office, but as a disguised conqueror. He had defeated I know not how many district-attorneys; he had dined at I know not how many public dinners; he had been heralded in I know not how many Weekly Arguses, and it was rumored that he had an army behind him and an empire before him. It was a great day—his arrival—to poor Nolan. Burr had not been at the fort an hour before he sent for him. That evening he asked Nolan to take him out in his skiff, to show him a canebrake or a cotton-wood tree, as he said,—really to seduce him; and by the time the sail was over Nolan was enlisted body and soul. From that time, though he did not yet know it, he lived as a man without a country.

What Burr meant to do I know no more than you, dear reader. It is none of our business just now. Only, when the grand catastrophe came, and Jefferson and the House of Virginia of that day undertook to break on the wheel all the possible Clarences of the then House of York, by the great treason-trial at Richmond, some of the lesser fry in that distant Mississippi Valley, which was farther from us than Puget's Sound is to-day, introduced the like novelty on their provincial stage, and, to while away the monotony of the summer at Fort Adams, got up, for *spectacles*, a string of court-martials on the officers there. One and another of the colonels and majors were tried, and, to fill out the list, little Nolan, against whom, Heaven knows, there was evidence enough,—that he was sick of the service, had been willing to be false to it, and would have obeyed any order to march any-whither with any one who would follow him, had the order only been signed, "By command of His Exc. A. Burr." The courts dragged on. The big flies escaped,—rightly for all I know. Nolan was proved guilty enough, as I say; yet you and I would never have heard of him, reader, but that, when the president of the court asked him at the close whether he wished to say anything to show that he hadalways been faithful to the United States, he cried out, in a fit of frenzy,—

"D—n the United States! I wish I may never hear of the United States again!"

I suppose he did not know how the words shocked old Colonel Morgan, who was holding the court. Half the officers who sat in it had served through the Revolution, and their lives, not to say their necks, had been risked for the very idea which he so cavalierly cursed in his madness. He, on his part, had grown up in the West of those days, in the midst of "Spanish plot," "Orleans plot," and all the rest. He had been educated on a plantation where the finest company was a Spanish officer or a French merchant from Orleans. His education, such as it was, had been perfected in commercial expeditions to Vera Cruz, and I think he told me his father once hired an Englishman to be a private tutor for a winter on the plantation. He had spent half his youth with an older brother, hunting horses in Texas; and, in a word, to him "United States" was scarcely a reality. Yet he had been fed by "United States" for all the years since he had been in the army. He had sworn on his faith as a Christian to be true to "United States." It was "United States" which gave him the uniform he wore, and the sword by his side. Nay, my poor Nolan, it was only because "United States" had picked you out first as one of her own confidential men of honor, that "A. Burr" cared for you a straw more than for the flat-boat men who sailed his ark for him. I do not excuse Nolan; I only explain to the reader why he damned his country, and wished he might never hear her name again.

He never did hear her name but once again. From that moment, September 23, 1807, till the day he died, May 11, 1863, he never heard her name again. For that half-century and more he was a man without a country.

Old Morgan, as I said, was terribly shocked. If Nolan had compared George Washington to Benedict Arnold, or had cried, "God save King George," Morgan would not have felt worse. He called the court into his private room, and returned in fifteen minutes, with a face like a sheet, to say,—

"Prisoner, hear the sentence of the Court! The Court decides, subject to the approval of the President, that you never hear the name of the United States again."

Nolan laughed. But nobody else laughed. Old Morgan was too solemn, and the whole room was hushed dead as night for a minute. Even Nolan lost his swagger in a moment. Then Morgan added,—

"Mr. Marshal, take the prisoner to Orleans in an armed boat, and deliver him to the naval commander there."

The Marshal gave his orders and the prisoner was taken out of court.

"Mr. Marshal," continued old Morgan, "see that no one mentions the United States to the prisoner. Mr. Marshal, make my respects to Lieutenant Mitchell at Orleans, and request him to order that no one shall mention the United States to the prisoner while he is on board ship. You will receive your written orders from the officer on duty here this evening. The court is adjourned without day."

I have always supposed that Colonel Morgan himselftook the proceedings of the court to Washington City, and explained them to Mr. Jefferson. Certain it is that the President approved them,—certain, that is, if I may believe the men who say they have seen his signature. Before the Nautilus got round from New Orleans to the Northern Atlantic coast with the prisoner on board, the sentence had been approved, and he was a man without a country.

The plan then adopted was substantially the same which was necessarily followed ever after. Perhaps it was suggested by the necessity of sending him by water from Fort Adams and Orleans. The Secretary of the Navy—it must have been the first Crowninshield, though he is a man I do not remember—was requested to put Nolan on board a government vessel bound on a long cruise, and to direct that he should be only so far confined there as to make it certain that he never saw or heard of the country. We had few long cruises then, and the navy was very much out of favor; and as almost all of this story is traditional, as I have explained, I do not know certainly what his first cruise was. But the commander to whom he was intrusted,—perhaps it was Tingey or Shaw, though I think it was one of the younger men,—we are all old enough now,—regulated the etiquette and the precautions of the affair, and according to his scheme they were carried out, I suppose, till Nolan died.

When I was second officer of the Intrepid, some thirty years after, I saw the original paper of instructions. I have been sorry ever since that I did not copy the whole of it. It ran, however, much in this way:—

"WASHINGTON" (with the date, which must have been late in 1807).

"SIR,—You will receive from Lieutenant Neale the person of Philip Nolan, late a Lieutenant in the United States Army.

"This person on his trial by court-martial expressed with an oath the wish that he might 'never hear of the United States again.'

"The Court sentenced him to have his wish fulfilled.

"For the present, the execution of the order is intrusted by the President to this department.

"You will take the prisoner on board your ship, and keep him there with such precautions as shall prevent his escape.

"You will provide him with such quarters, rations, and clothing as would be proper for an officer of his late rank, if he were a passenger on your vessel on the business of his government.

"The gentlemen on board will make any arrangements agreeable to themselves regarding his society. He is to be exposed to no indignity of any kind, nor is he ever unnecessarily to be reminded that he is a prisoner.

"But under no circumstances is he ever to hear of his country or to see any information regarding it; and you will specially caution all the officers under your command to take care, that in the various indulgences which may be granted, this rule, in which his punishment is involved, shall not be broken.

"It is the intention of the government that he shall never again see the country which he has disowned.Before the end of your cruise you will receive orders which will give effect to this intention.

"Respectfully yours,
"W. SOUTHARD, for the
Secretary of the Navy."

If I had only preserved the whole of this paper, there would be no break in the beginning of my sketch of this story. For Captain Shaw, if it was he, handed it to his successor in the charge, and he to his, and I suppose the commander of the Levant has it to-day as his authority for keeping this man in this mild custody.

The rule adopted on board the ships on which I have met "the man without a country" was, I think, transmitted from the beginning. No mess liked to have him permanently, because his presence cut off all talk of home or of the prospect of return, of politics or letters, of peace or of war,—cut off more than half the talk men like to have at sea. But it was always thought too hard that he should never meet the rest of us, except to touch hats, and we finally sank into one system. He was not permitted to talk with the men, unless an officer was by. With officers he had unrestrained intercourse, as far as they and he chose. But he grew shy, though he had favorites: I was one. Then the captain always asked him to dinner on Monday. Every mess in succession took up the invitation in its turn. According to the size of the ship, you had him at your mess more or less often at dinner. His breakfast he ate in his own state-room,—he always had a state-room,—which was where a sentinel or somebody on the watch could see the door. Andwhatever else he ate or drank, he ate or drank alone. Sometimes, when the marines or sailors had any special jollification, they were permitted to invite "Plain-Buttons," as they called him. Then Nolan was sent with some officer, and the men were forbidden to speak of home while he was there. I believe the theory was that the sight of his punishment did them good. They called him "Plain-Buttons," because, while he always chose to wear a regulation army-uniform, he was not permitted to wear the army-button, for the reason that it bore either the initials or the insignia of the country he had disowned.

I remember, soon after I joined the navy, I was on shore with some of the older officers from our ship and from the Brandywine, which we had met at Alexandria. We had leave to make a party and go up to Cairo and the Pyramids. As we jogged along (you went on donkeys then), some of the gentlemen (we boys called them "Dons," but the phrase was long since changed) fell to talking about Nolan, and some one told the system which was adopted from the first about his books and other reading. As he was almost never permitted to go on shore, even though the vessel lay in port for months, his time, at the best, hung heavy; and everybody was permitted to lend him books, if they were not published in America and made no allusion to it. These were common enough in the old days, when people in the other hemisphere talked of the United States as little as we do of Paraguay. He had almost all the foreign papers that came into the ship, sooner or later; only somebody must go over them first, and cut out any advertisement or stray paragraph that alluded to America. This was a little cruel sometimes, when the back of what was cut out might be as innocent as Hesiod. Right in the midst of one of Napoleon's battles, or one of Canning's speeches, poor Nolan would find a great hole, because on the back of the page of that paper there had been an advertisement of a packet for New York, or a scrap from the President's message. I say this was the first time I ever heard of this plan, which afterwards I had enough, and more than enough to do with. I remember it, because poor Phillips, who was of the party, as soon as the allusion to reading was made, told a story of something which happened at the Cape of Good Hope on Nolan's first voyage; and it is the only thing I ever knew of that voyage. They had touched at the Cape, and had done the civil thing with the English Admiral and the fleet, and then, leaving for a long cruise up the Indian Ocean, Phillips had borrowed a lot of English books from an officer, which, in those days, as indeed in these, was quite a windfall. Among them, as the Devil would order, was the "Lay of the Last Minstrel," which they had all of them heard of, but which most of them had never seen. I think it could not have been published long. Well, nobody thought there could be any risk of anything national in that, though Phillips swore old Shaw had cut out the "Tempest" from Shakespeare before he let Nolan have it, because he said "the Bermudas ought to be ours, and, by Jove, should be one day." So Nolan was permitted to join the circle one afternoon when a lot of them sat on deck smoking and reading aloud. People do not do such things so often now; but when I wasyoung we got rid of a great deal of time so. Well, so it happened that in his turn Nolan took the book and read to the others; and he read very well, as I know. Nobody in the circle knew a line of the poem, only it was all magic and Border chivalry, and was ten thousand years ago. Poor Nolan read steadily through the fifth canto, stopped a minute and drank something, and then began, without a thought of what was coming,—

"Breathes there the man, with soul so dead,

Who never to himself hath said—"

It seems impossible to us that anybody ever heard this for the first time; but all these fellows did then, and poor Nolan himself went on, still unconsciously or mechanically,—

"This is my own, my native land!"

Then they all saw something was to pay; but he expected to get through, I suppose, turned a little pale, but plunged on,—

"Whose heart hath ne'er within him burned,

As home his footsteps he hath turned

From wandering on a foreign strand?—

If such there breathe, go, mark him well."

By this time the men were all beside themselves, wishing there was any way to make him turn over two pages; but he had not quite presence of mind for that; he gagged a little, colored crimson, and staggered on,—

"For him no minstrel raptures swell;

High though his titles, proud his name,

Boundless his wealth as wish can claim,

Despite these titles, power, and pelf,

The wretch, concentred all in self—"

and here the poor fellow choked, could not go on, but started up, swung the book into the sea, vanished into his state-room, "And by Jove," said Phillips, "we did not see him for two months again. And I had to make up some beggarly story to that English surgeon why I did not return his Walter Scott to him."

That story shows about the time when Nolan's braggadocio must have broken down. At first, they said, he took a very high tone, considered his imprisonment a mere farce, affected to enjoy the voyage, and all that; but Phillips said that after he came out of his state-room he never was the same man again. He never read aloud again, unless it was the Bible or Shakespeare, or something else he was sure of. But it was not that merely. He never entered in with the other young men exactly as a companion again. He was always shy afterwards, when I knew him,—very seldom spoke unless he was spoken to, except to a very few friends. He lighted up occasionally,—I remember late in his life hearing him fairly eloquent on something which had been suggested to him by one of Fléchier's sermons,—but generally he had the nervous, tired look of a heart-wounded man.

When Captain Shaw was coming home,—if, as I say, it was Shaw,—rather to the surprise of everybody they made one of the Windward Islands, and lay off and on for nearly a week. The boys said the officers were sick of salt-junk, and meant to have turtle-soup before they came home. But after several days the Warren came to the same rendezvous; they exchanged signals;she sent to Phillips and these homeward-bound men letters and papers, and told them she was outward-bound, perhaps to the Mediterranean, and took poor Nolan and his traps on the boat back to try his second cruise. He looked very blank when he was told to get ready to join her. He had known enough of the signs of the sky to know that till that moment he was going "home." But this was a distinct evidence of something he had not thought of, perhaps,—that there was no going home for him, even to a prison. And this was the first of some twenty such transfers, which brought him sooner or later into half our best vessels, but which kept him all his life at least some hundred miles from the country he had hoped he might never hear of again.

It may have been on that second cruise—it was once when he was up the Mediterranean—that Mrs. Graff, the celebrated Southern beauty of those days, danced with him. They had been lying a long time in the Bay of Naples, and the officers were very intimate in the English fleet, and there had been great festivities, and our men thought they must give a great ball on board the ship. How they ever did it on board the Warren I am sure I do not know. Perhaps it was not the Warren, or perhaps ladies did not take up so much room as they do now. They wanted to use Nolan's state-room for something, and they hated to do it without asking him to the ball; so the captain said they might ask him, if they would be responsible that he did not talk with the wrong people, "who would give him intelligence." So the dance went on, the finest party that had ever been known, I dare say; for I never heard of a man-of-warball that was not. For ladies they had the family of the American consul, one or two travellers who had adventured so far, and a nice bevy of English girls and matrons, perhaps Lady Hamilton herself.

Well, different officers relieved each other in standing and talking with Nolan in a friendly way, so as to be sure that nobody else spoke to him. The dancing went on with spirit, and after a while even the fellows who took this honorary guard of Nolan ceased to fear any *contre-temps*. Only when some English lady—Lady Hamilton, as I said, perhaps—called for a set of "American dances," an odd thing happened. Everybody then danced contra-dances. The black band, nothing loath, conferred as to what "American dances" were, and started off with "Virginia Reel," which they followed with "Money-Musk," which in its turn in those days should have been followed by "The Old Thirteen." But just as Dick, the leader, tapped for his fiddles to begin, and bent forward, about to say in true negro state, "'The Old Thirteen,' gentlemen and ladies!" as he had said "'Virginny Reel,' if you please!" and "'Money-Musk,' if you please!" the captain's boy tapped him on the shoulder, whispered to him, and he did not announce the name of the dance; he merely bowed, began on the air, and they all fell to,—the officers teaching the English girls the figure, but not telling them why it had no name.

But that is not the story I started to tell.—As the dancing went on, Nolan and our fellows all got at ease, as I said,—so much so, that it seemed quite natural for him to bow to that splendid Mrs. Graff, and say,—

"I hope you have not forgotten me, Miss Rutledge. Shall I have the honor of dancing?"

He did it so quickly, that Fellows, who was by him, could not hinder him. She laughed, and said,—

"I am not Miss Rutledge any longer, Mr. Nolan; but I will dance all the same," just nodded to Fellows, as if to say he must leave Mr. Nolan to her, and led him off to the place where the dance was forming.

Nolan thought he had got his chance. He had known her at Philadelphia, and at other places had met her, and this was a Godsend. You could not talk in contra-dances, as you do in cotillons, or even in the pauses of waltzing; but there were chances for tongues and sounds, as well as for eyes and blushes. He began with her travels, and Europe, and Vesuvius, and the French; and then, when they had worked down, and had that long talking-time at the bottom of the set, he said boldly,—a little pale, she said, as she told me the story, years after,—

"And what do you hear from home, Mrs. Graff?"

And that splendid creature looked through him. Jove! how she must have looked through him!

"Home!! Mr. Nolan!!! I thought you were the man who never wanted to hear of home again!"—And she walked directly up the deck to her husband, and left poor Nolan alone, as he always was.—He did not dance again.

I cannot give any history of him in order; nobody can now; and, indeed, I am not trying to. These are the traditions, which I sort out, as I believe them, from the myths which have been told about this man for fortyyears. The lies that have been told about him are legion. The fellows used to say he was the "Iron Mask"; and poor George Pons went to his grave in the belief that this was the author of "Junius," who was being punished for his celebrated libel on Thomas Jefferson. Pons was not very strong in the historical line. A happier story than either of these I have told is of the War. That came along soon after. I have heard this affair told in three or four ways,—and indeed it may have happened more than once. But which ship it was on I cannot tell. However, in one, at least, of the great frigate-duels with the English, in which the navy was really baptized, it happened that a round-shot from the enemy entered one of our ports square, and took right down the officer of the gun himself, and almost every man of the gun's crew. Now you may say what you choose about courage, but that is not a nice thing to see. But, as the men who were not killed picked themselves up, and as they and the surgeon's people were carrying off the bodies, there appeared Nolan, in his shirt-sleeves, with the rammer in his hand, and, just as if he had been the officer, told them off with authority,—who should go to the cockpit with the wounded men, who should stay with him,—perfectly cheery, and with that way which makes men feel sure all is right and is going to be right. And he finished loading the gun with his own hands, aimed it, and bade the men fire. And there he stayed, captain of that gun, keeping those fellows in spirits, till the enemy struck,—sitting on the carriage while the gun was cooling, though he was exposed all the time,—showing them easier ways to handle heavyshot,—making the raw hands laugh at their own blunders,—and when the gun cooled again, getting it loaded and fired twice as often as any other gun on the ship. The captain walked forward by way of encouraging the men, and Nolan touched his hat and said,—

"I am showing them how we do this in the artillery, sir."

And this is the part of the story where all the legends agree; that the Commodore said,—

"I see you do, and I thank you, sir; and I shall never forget this day, sir, and you never shall, sir."

And after the whole thing was over, and he had the Englishman's sword, in the midst of the state and ceremony of the quarter-deck, he said,—

"Where is Mr. Nolan? Ask Mr. Nolan to come here."

And when Nolan came the captain said,—

"Mr. Nolan, we are all very grateful to you to-day; you are one of us to-day; you will be named in the despatches."

And then the old man took off his own sword of ceremony, and gave it to Nolan, and made him put it on. The man told me this who saw it. Nolan cried like a baby, and well he might. He had not worn a sword since that infernal day at Fort Adams. But always afterwards, on occasions of ceremony, he wore that quaint old French sword of the Commodore's.

The captain did mention him in the despatches. It was always said he asked that he might be pardoned. He wrote a special letter to the Secretary of War. But nothing ever came of it. As I said, that was about thetime when they began to ignore the whole transaction at Washington, and when Nolan's imprisonment began to carry itself on because there was nobody to stop it without any new orders from home.

I have heard it said that he was with Porter when he took possession of the Nukahiwa Islands. Not this Porter, you know, but old Porter, his father, Essex Porter,—that is, the old Essex Porter, not this Essex. As an artillery officer, who had seen service in the West, Nolan knew more about fortifications, embrasures, ravelins, stockades, and all that, than any of them did; and he worked with a right good-will in fixing that battery all right. I have always thought it was a pity Porter did not leave him in command there with Gamble. That would have settled all the question about his punishment. We should have kept the islands, and at this moment we should have one station in the Pacific Ocean. Our French friends, too, when they wanted this little watering-place, would have found it was preoccupied. But Madison and the Virginians, of course, flung all that away.

All that was near fifty years ago. If Nolan was thirty then, he must have been near eighty when he died. He looked sixty when he was forty. But he never seemed to me to change a hair afterwards. As I imagine his life, from what I have seen and heard of it, he must have been in every sea, and yet almost never on land. He must have known, in a formal way, more officers in our service than any man living knows. He told me once, with a grave smile, that no man in the world lived so methodical a life as he. "You know the boys say I amthe Iron Mask, and you know how busy he was." He said it did not do for any one to try to read all the time, more than to do anything else all the time; but that he read just five hours a day. "Then," he said, "I keep up my note-books, writing in them at such and such hours from what I have been reading; and I include in these my scrap-books." These were very curious indeed. He had six or eight, of different subjects. There was one of History, one of Natural Science, one which he called "Odds and Ends." But they were not merely books of extracts from newspapers. They had bits of plants and ribbons, shells tied on, and carved scraps of bone and wood, which he had taught the men to cut for him, and they were beautifully illustrated. He drew admirably. He had some of the funniest drawings there, and some of the most pathetic, that I have ever seen in my life. I wonder who will have Nolan's scrap-books.

Well, he said his reading and his notes were his profession, and that they took five hours and two hours respectively of each day. "Then," said he, "every man should have a diversion as well as a profession. My Natural History is my diversion." That took two hours a day more. The men used to bring him birds and fish, but on a long cruise he had to satisfy himself with centipedes and cockroaches and such small game. He was the only naturalist I ever met who knew anything about the habits of the house-fly and the mosquito. All those people can tell you whether they are *Lepidoptera* or *Steptopotera*; but as for telling how you can get rid of them, or how they get away from you when you strikethem,—why, Linnæus knew as little of that as John Foy the idiot did. These nine hours made Nolan's regular daily "occupation." The rest of the time he talked or walked. Till he grew very old, he went aloft a great deal. He always kept up his exercise; and I never heard that he was ill. If any other man was ill, he was the kindest nurse in the world; and he knew more than half the surgeons do. Then if anybody was sick or died, or if the captain wanted him to on any other occasion, he was always ready to read prayers. I have said that he read beautifully.

My own acquaintance with Philip Nolan began six or eight years after the War, on my first voyage after I was appointed a midshipman. It was in the first days after our Slave-Trade treaty, while the Reigning House, which was still the House of Virginia, had still a sort of sentimentalism about the suppression of the horrors of the Middle Passage, and something was sometimes done that way. We were in the South Atlantic on that business. From the time I joined, I believe I thought Nolan was a sort of lay chaplain,—a chaplain with a blue coat. I never asked about him. Everything in the ship was strange to me. I knew it was green to ask questions, and I suppose I thought there was a "Plain Buttons" on every ship. We had him to dine in our mess once a week, and the caution was given that on that day nothing was to be said about home. But if they had told us not to say anything about the planet Mars or the Book of Deuteronomy, I should not have asked why; there were a great many things which seemed to me to have as little reason. I first came tounderstand anything about "the man without a country" one day when we overhauled a dirty little schooner which had slaves on board. An officer was sent to take charge of her, and, after a few minutes, he sent back his boat to ask that some one might be sent him who could speak Portuguese. We were all looking over the rail when the message came, and we all wished we could interpret, when the captain asked who spoke Portuguese. But none of the officers did; and just as the captain was sending forward to ask if any of the people could, Nolan stepped out and said he should be glad to interpret, if the captain wished, as he understood the language. The captain thanked him, fitted out another boat with him, and in this boat it was my luck to go.

When we got there, it was such a scene as you seldom see, and never want to. Nastiness beyond account, and chaos run loose in the midst of the nastiness. There were not a great many of the negroes; but by way of making what there were understand that they were free, Vaughan had had their hand-cuffs and ankle-cuffs knocked off, and, for convenience' sake was putting them upon the rascals of the schooner's crew. The negroes were, most of them, out of the hold, and swarming all round the dirty deck, with a central throng surrounding Vaughan and addressing him in every dialect and *patois* of a dialect, from the Zulu click up to the Parisian of Beledeljereed.

As we came on deck, Vaughan looked down from a hogshead, on which he had mounted in desperation, and said,—

"For God's love, is there anybody who can makethese wretches understand something? The men gave them rum, and that did not quiet them. I knocked that big fellow down twice, and that did not soothe him. And then I talked Choctaw to all of them together; and I'll be hanged if they understood that as well as they understood the English."

Nolan said he could speak Portuguese, and one or two fine-looking Kroomen were dragged out, who, as it had been found already, had worked for the Portuguese on the coast at Fernando Po.

"Tell them they are free," said Vaughan; "and tell them that these rascals are to be hanged as soon as we can get rope enough."

Nolan "put that into Spanish,"—that is, he explained it in such Portuguese as the Kroomen could understand, and they in turn to such of the negroes as could understand them. Then there was such a yell of delight, clinching of fists, leaping and dancing, kissing of Nolan's feet, and a general rush made to the hogshead by way of spontaneous worship of Vaughan, as the *deus ex machina* of the occasion.

"Tell them," said Vaughan, well pleased, "that I will take them all to Cape Palmas."

This did not answer so well. Cape Palmas was practically as far from the homes of most of them as New Orleans or Rio Janeiro was; that is, they would be eternally separated from home there. And their interpreters, as we could understand, instantly said, "*Ah, non Palmas,*" and began to propose infinite other expedients in most voluble language. Vaughan was rather disappointed at this result of his liberality, and askedNolan eagerly what they said. The drops stood on poor Nolan's white forehead, as he hushed the men down, and said,—

"He says, 'Not Palmas.' He says, 'Take us home, take us to our own country, take us to our own house, take us to our own pickaninnies and our own women.' He says he has an old father and mother who will die if they do not see him. And this one says he left his people all sick, and paddled down to Fernando to beg the white doctor to come and help them, and that these devils caught him in the bay just in sight of home, and that he has never seen anybody from home since then. And this one says," choked out Nolan, "that he has not heard a word from his home in six months, while he has been locked up in an infernal barracoon."

Vaughan always said he grew gray himself while Nolan struggled through this interpretation. I, who did not understand anything of the passion involved in it, saw that the very elements were melting with fervent heat, and that something was to pay somewhere. Even the negroes themselves stopped howling, as they saw Nolan's agony, and Vaughan's almost equal agony of sympathy. As quick as he could get words he said,—

"Tell them yes, yes, yes; tell them they shall go to the Mountains of the Moon, if they will. If I sail the schooner through the Great White Desert, they shall go home!"

And after some fashion Nolan said so. And then they all fell to kissing him again, and wanted to rub his nose with theirs.

But he could not stand it long; and getting Vaughanto say he might go back, he beckoned me down into our boat. As we lay back in the stern-sheets and the men gave way, he said to me, "Youngster, let that show you what it is to be without a family, without a home, and without a country. And if you are ever tempted to say a word or to do a thing that shall put a bar between you and your family, your home, and your country, pray God in his mercy to take you that instant home to his own heaven. Stick by your family, boy; forget you have a self, while you do everything for them. Think of your home, boy; write and send, and talk about it. Let it be nearer and nearer to your thought, the farther you have to travel from it; and rush back to it, when you are free, as that poor black slave is doing now. And for your country, boy," and the words rattled in his throat, "and for that flag," and he pointed to the ship, "never dream a dream but of serving her as she bids you, though the service carry you through a thousand hells. No matter what happens to you, no matter who flatters you or who abuses you, never look at another flag, never let a night pass but you pray God to bless that flag. Remember, boy, that behind all these men you have to do with, behind officers, and government, and people even, there is the Country Herself, your Country, and that you belong to Her as you belong to your own mother. Stand by Her, boy, as you would stand by your mother, if those devils there had got hold of her to-day!"

I was frightened to death by his calm, hard passion; but I blundered out, that I would, by all that was holy, and that I had never thought of doing anything else. He hardly seemed to hear me; but he did, almost in awhisper, say, "O, if anybody had said so to me when I was of your age!"

I think it was this half-confidence of his, which I never abused, for I never told this story till now, which afterward made us great friends. He was very kind to me. Often he sat up, or even got up, at night, to walk the deck with me, when it was my watch. He explained to me a great deal of my mathematics, and I owe to him my taste for mathematics. He lent me books, and helped me about my reading. He never alluded so directly to his story again; but from one and another officer I have learned, in thirty years, what I am telling. When we parted from him in St. Thomas Harbor, at the end of our cruise, I was more sorry than I can tell. I was very glad to meet him again in 1830; and later in life, when I thought I had some influence in Washington, I moved heaven and earth to have him discharged. But it was like getting a ghost out of prison. They pretended there was no such man, and never was such a man. They will say so at the Department now! Perhaps they do not know. It will not be the first thing in the service of which the Department appears to know nothing!

There is a story that Nolan met Burr, once on one of our vessels, when a party of Americans came on board in the Mediterranean. But this I believe to be a lie; or, rather, it is a myth, *ben trovato*, involving a tremendous blowing-up with which he sunk Burr,—asking him how he liked to be "without a country." But it is clear, from Burr's life, that nothing of the sort could have happened; and I mention this only as an illustration of the stories which get a-going where there is the least mystery at bottom.

So poor Philip Nolan had his wish fulfilled. I know but one fate more dreadful: it is the fate reserved for those men who shall have one day to exile themselves from their country because they have attempted her ruin, and shall have at the same time to see the prosperity and honor to which she rises when she has rid herself of them and their iniquities. The wish of poor Nolan, as we all learned to call him, not because his punishment was too great, but because his repentance was so clear, was precisely the wish of every Bragg and Beauregard who broke a soldier's oath two years ago, and of every Maury and Barron who broke a sailor's. I do not know how often they have repented. I do know that they have done all that in them lay that they might have no country,—that all the honors, associations, memories, and hopes which belong to "country" might be broken up into little shreds and distributed to the winds. I know, too, that their punishment, as they vegetate through what is left of life to them in wretched Boulognes and Leicester Squares, where they are destined to upbraid each other till they die, will have all the agony of Nolan's, with the added pang that every one who sees them will see them to despise and to execrate them. They will have their wish, like him.

For him, poor fellow, he repented of his folly, and then, like a man, submitted to the fate he had asked for. He never intentionally added to the difficulty or delicacy of the charge of those who had him in hold. Accidents would happen; but they never happened from his fault. Lieutenant Truxton told me, that, when Texas was annexed, there was a careful discussion among the officers,whether they should get hold of Nolan's handsome set of maps and cut Texas out of it,—from the map of the world and the map of Mexico. The United States had been cut out when the atlas was bought for him. But it was voted rightly enough, that to do this would be virtually to reveal to him what had happened, or, as Harry Cole said, to make him think old Burr had succeeded. So it was from no fault of Nolan's that a great botch happened at my own table, when, for a short time, I was in command of the George Washington corvette, on the South American station. We were lying in the La Plata, and some of the officers, who had been on shore, and had just joined again, were entertaining us with accounts of their misadventures in riding the half-wild horses of Buenos Ayres. Nolan was at table, and was in an unusually bright and talkative mood. Some story of a tumble reminded him of an adventure of his own, when he was catching wild horses in Texas with his brother Stephen, at a time when he must have been quite a boy. He told the story with a good deal of spirit,—so much so, that the silence which often follows a good story hung over the table for an instant, to be broken by Nolan himself. For he asked, perfectly unconsciously,—

"Pray, what has become of Texas? After the Mexicans got their independence, I thought that province of Texas would come forward very fast. It is really one of the finest regions on earth; it is the Italy of this continent. But I have not seen or heard a word of Texas for near twenty years."

There were two Texan officers at the table. The reason he had never heard of Texas was that Texas and her affairs had been painfully cut out of his newspapers since Austin began his settlements; so that, while he read of Honduras and Tamaulipas, and till quite lately, of California,—this virgin province, in which his brother had travelled so far, and, I believe, had died, had ceased to be to him. Waters and Williams, the two Texas men, looked grimly at each other, and tried not to laugh. Edward Morris had his attention attracted by the third link in the chain of the captain's chandelier. Watrous was seized with a convulsion of sneezing. Nolan himself saw that something was to pay, he did not know what. And I, as master of the feast, had to say,—

"Texas is out of the map, Mr. Nolan. Have you seen Captain Back's curious account of Sir Thomas Roe's Welcome?"

After that cruise I never saw Nolan again. I wrote to him at least twice a year, for in that voyage we became even confidentially intimate; but he never wrote to me. The other men tell me that in those fifteen years he *aged* very fast, as well he might indeed, but that he was still the same gentle, uncomplaining, silent sufferer that he ever was, bearing as best he could his self-appointed punishment,—rather less social, perhaps, with new men whom he did not know, but more anxious, apparently, than ever to serve and befriend and teach the boys, some of whom fairly seemed to worship him. And now, it seems, the dear old fellow is dead. He has found a home at last, and a country.

Since writing this, and while considering whether or no I would print it, as a warning to the young Nolansand Vallandighams and Tatnals of to-day of what it is to throw away a country, I have received from Danforth, who is on board the Levant, a letter which gives an account of Nolan's last hours. It removes all my doubts about telling this story.

To understand the first words of the letter, the nonprofessional reader should remember that after 1817, the position of every officer who had Nolan in charge was one of the greatest delicacy. The government had failed to renew the order of 1807 regarding him. What was a man to do? Should he let him go? What, then, if he were called to account by the Department for violating the order of 1807? Should he keep him? What, then, if Nolan should be liberated some day, and should bring an action for false imprisonment or kidnapping against every man who had had him in charge? I urged and pressed this upon Southard, and I have reason to think that other officers did the same thing. But the Secretary always said, as they so often do at Washington, that there were no special orders to give, and that we must act on our own judgment. That means, "If you succeed, you will be sustained; if you fail, you will be disavowed." Well, as Danforth says, all that is over now, though I do not know but I expose myself to a criminal prosecution on the evidence of the very revelation I am making.

Here is the letter:—

LEVANT, 2° 2' S. @ 131° W.

"DEAR FRED,—I try to find heart and life to tell you that it is all over with dear old Nolan. I have been with him on this voyage more than I ever was, and I can understand wholly now the way in which you used to speakof the dear old fellow. I could see that he was not strong, but I had no idea the end was so near. The doctor has been watching him very carefully, and yesterday morning came to me and told me that Nolan was not so well, and had not left his state-room,—a thing I never remember before. He had let the doctor come and see him as he lay there,—the first time the doctor had been in the state-room,—and he said he should like to see me. O dear! do you remember the mysteries we boys used to invent about his room, in the old Intrepid days? Well, I went in, and there, to be sure, the poor fellow lay in his berth, smiling pleasantly as he gave me his hand, but looking very frail. I could not help a glance round, which showed me what a little shrine he had made of the box he was lying in. The stars and stripes were triced up above and around a picture of Washington, and he had painted a majestic eagle, with lightnings blazing from his beak and his foot just clasping the whole globe, which his wings overshadowed. The dear old boy saw my glance, and said, with a sad smile, 'Here, you see, I have a country!' And then he pointed to the foot of his bed, where I had not seen before a great map of the United States, as he had drawn it from memory, and which he had there to look upon as he lay. Quaint, queer old names were on it, in large letters: 'Indiana Territory,' 'Mississippi Territory,' and 'Louisiana Territory,' as I suppose our fathers learned such things: but the old fellow had patched in Texas, too; he had carried his western boundary all the way to the Pacific, but on that shore he had defined nothing.

"'O Danforth,' he said, 'I know I am dying. I cannot get home. Surely you will tell me something now?—Stop! stop! Do not speak till I say what I am sure you know, that there is not in this ship, that there is not in America,—God bless her!—a more loyal man than I. There cannot be a man who loves the old flag as I do, or prays for it as I do, or hopes for it as I do. There are thirty-four stars in it now, Danforth. I thank God for that, though I do not know what their names are. There has never been one taken away: I thank God for that. I know by that, that there has never been any successful Burr. O Danforth, Danforth,' he sighed out, 'how like a wretched night's dream a boy's idea of personal fame or of separate sovereignty seems, when one looks back on it after such a life as mine! But tell me,—tell me something,—tell me everything, Danforth, before I die!'

"Ingham, I swear to you that I felt like a monster that I had not told him everything before. Danger or no danger, delicacy or no delicacy, who was I, that I should have been acting the tyrant all this time over this dear, sainted old man, who had years ago expiated, in his whole manhood's life, the madness of a boy's treason? 'Mr. Nolan,' said I, 'I will tell you everything you ask about. Only, where shall I begin?'

"O the blessed smile that crept over his white face! and he pressed my hand and said, 'God bless you!' 'Tell me their names,' he said, and he pointed to the stars on the flag. 'The last I know is Ohio. My father lived in Kentucky. But I have guessed Michigan and Indiana and Mississippi,—that was where Fort Adams is,—they make twenty. But where are yourother fourteen? You have not cut up any of the old ones, I hope?'

"Well, that was not a bad text, and I told him the names in as good order as I could, and he bade me take down his beautiful map and draw them in as I best could with my pencil. He was wild with delight about Texas, told me how his brother died there; he had marked a gold cross where he supposed his brother's grave was; and he had guessed at Texas. Then he was delighted as he saw California and Oregon;—that, he said, he had suspected partly, because he had never been permitted to land on that shore, though the ships were there so much. 'And the men,' said he, laughing, 'brought off a good deal besides furs.' Then he went back—heavens, how far!—to ask about the Chesapeake, and what was done to Barron for surrendering her to the Leopard, and whether Burr ever tried again,—and he ground his teeth with the only passion he showed. But in a moment that was over, and he said, 'God forgive me, for I am sure I forgive him.' Then he asked about the old war,—told me the true story of his serving the gun the day we took the Java,—asked about dear old David Porter, as he called him. Then he settled down more quietly, and very happily, to hear me tell in an hour the history of fifty years.

"How I wished it had been somebody who knew something! But I did as well as I could. I told him of the English war. I told him about Fulton and the steamboat beginning. I told him about old Scott, and Jackson; told him all I could think about the Mississippi, and New Orleans, and Texas, and his own oldKentucky. And do you think, he asked, who was in command of the 'Legion of the West.' I told him it was a very gallant officer named Grant, and that, by our last news, he was about to establish his head-quarters at Vicksburg. Then, 'Where was Vicksburg?' I worked that out on the map; it was about a hundred miles, more or less, above his old Fort Adams; and I thought Fort Adams must be a ruin now. 'It must be at old Vick's plantation,' said he; 'well, that is a change!'

"I tell you, Ingham, it was a hard thing to condense the history of half a century into that talk with a sick man. And I do not now know what I told him,—of emigration, and the means of it,—of steamboats, and railroads, and telegraphs,—of inventions, and books, and literature,—of the colleges, and West Point, and the Naval School,—but with the queerest interruptions that ever you heard. You see it was Robinson Crusoe asking all the accumulated questions of fifty-six years!

"I remember he asked, all of a sudden, who was President now; and when I told him, he asked if Old Abe was General Benjamin Lincoln's son. He said he met old General Lincoln, when he was quite a boy himself, at some Indian treaty. I said no, that Old Abe was a Kentuckian like himself, but I could not tell him of what family; he had worked up from the ranks. 'Good for him!' cried Nolan; 'I am glad of that. As I have brooded and wondered, I have thought our danger was in keeping up those regular successions in the first families.' Then I got talking about my visit to Washington. I told him of meeting the

Oregon Congressman, Harding; I told him about the Smithsonian, and the ExploringExpedition; I told him about the Capitol, and the statues for the pediment, and Crawford's Liberty, and Greenough's Washington. Ingham, I told him everything I could think of that would show the grandeur of his country and its prosperity; but I could not make up my mouth to tell him a word about this infernal Rebellion!

"And he drank it in, and enjoyed it as I cannot tell you. He grew more and more silent, yet I never thought he was tired or faint. I gave him a glass of water, but he just wet his lips, and told me not to go away. Then he asked me to bring the Presbyterian 'Book of Public Prayer,' which lay there, and said, with a smile, that it would open at the right place,—and so it did. There was his double red mark down the page; and I knelt down and read, and he repeated with me, 'For ourselves and our country, O gracious God, we thank Thee, that notwithstanding our manifold transgressions of Thy holy laws, Thou hast continued to us Thy marvellous kindness,'—and so to the end of that thanksgiving. Then he turned to the end of the same book, and I read the words more familiar to me,—'Most heartily we beseech Thee with Thy favor to behold and bless Thy servant, the President of the United States, and all others in authority,'—and the rest of the Episcopal Collect. 'Danforth,' said he, 'I have repeated those prayers night and morning, it is now fifty-five years.' And then he said he would go to sleep. He bent me down over him and kissed me; and he said, 'Look in my Bible, Danforth, when I am gone.' And I went away.

"But I had no thought it was the end. I thought hewas tired and would sleep. I knew he was happy and I wanted him to be alone.

"But in an hour, when the doctor went in gently, he found Nolan had breathed his life away with a smile. He had something pressed close to his lips. It was his father's badge of the Order of Cincinnati.

"We looked in his Bible, and there was a slip of paper, at the place where he had marked the text,—

"'They desire a country, even a heavenly: wherefore God is not ashamed to be called their God: for he hath prepared for them a city.'

"On this slip of paper he had written,—

"'Bury me in the sea; it has been my home, and I love it. But will not some one set up a stone for my memory at Fort Adams or at Orleans, that my disgrace may not be more than I ought to bear? Say on it,—

"'IN MEMORY OF
"'PHILIP NOLAN
"'LIEUTENANT IN THE ARMY OF THE UNITED STATES.

"'He loved his country as no other man has loved her; but no man deserved less at her hands.'"

FLIGHT OF A TARTAR TRIBE.

BY THOMAS DE QUINCEY.

There is no great event in modern history, or, perhaps it may be said more broadly, none in all history, from its earliest records, less generally known, or more striking to the imagination, than the flight eastward of a principal Tartar nation across the boundless *steppes* of Asia in the latter half of the last century. The *terminus a quo* of this flight and the *terminus ad quem* are equally magnificent,—the mightiest of Christian thrones being the one, the mightiest of pagan the other; and the grandeur of these two terminal objects is harmoniously supported by the romantic circumstances of the flight. In the abruptness of its commencement and the fierce velocity of its execution we read an expression of the wild, barbaric character of the agents. In the unity of purpose connecting this myriad of wills, and in the blind but unerring aim at a mark so remote, there is something which recalls to the mind those almighty instincts that propel the migrations of the swallow or the life-withering marches of the locust. Then, again, in the gloomy vengeance of Russia and her vast artillery, which hung upon the rear and the skirtsof the fugitive vassals, we are reminded of Miltonic images,—such, for instance, as that of the solitary hand pursuing through desert spaces and through ancient chaos a rebellious host, and overtaking with volleying thunders those who believed themselves already within the security of darkness and of distance.

We shall have occasion, farther on, to compare this event with other great national catastrophes as to the magnitude of the suffering; but it may also challenge a comparison with similar events under another relation, viz. as to its dramatic capabilities. Few cases, perhaps, in romance or history, can sustain a close collation with this as to the complexity of its separate interests. The great outline of the enterprise, taken in connection with the operative motives, hidden or avowed, and the religious sanctions under which it was pursued, give to the case a triple character: 1st. That of a conspiracy, with as close a unity in the incidents, and as much of a personal interest in the moving characters, with fine dramatic contrasts, as belongs to Venice Preserved or to the Fiesco of Schiller. 2dly. That of a great military expedition, offering the same romantic features of vast distances to be traversed, vast reverses to be sustained, untried routes, enemies obscurely ascertained, and hardships too vaguely prefigured, which mark the Egyptian expedition of Cambyses; the anabasis of the younger Cyrus, and the subsequent retreat of the ten thousand to the Black Sea; the Parthian expeditions of the Romans, especially those of Crassus and Julian; or (as more disastrous than any of them, and in point of space, as well as in amount of forces, more extensive) the Russian anabasis and katabasis of Napoleon. 3dly. That of a religious exodus, authorized by an oracle venerated throughout many nations of Asia,—an exodus therefore, in so far resembling the great scriptural exodus of the Israelites under Moses and Joshua, as well as in the very peculiar distinction of carrying along with them their entire families, women, children, slaves, their herds of cattle and of sheep, their horses and their camels.

This triple character of the enterprise naturally invests it with a more comprehensive interest; but the dramatic interest which we ascribed to it, or its fitness for a stage representation, depends partly upon the marked variety and the strength of the personal agencies concerned, and partly upon the succession of scenical situations. Even the *steppes*, the camels, the tents, the snowy and the sandy deserts, are not beyond the scale of our modern representative powers, as often called into action in the theatres both of Paris and London; and the series of situations unfolded, beginning with the general conflagration on the Wolga; passing thence to the disastrous scenes of the flight (as it literally was in its commencement); to the Tartar siege of the Russian fortress Koulagina; the bloody engagement with the Cossacks in the mountain passes at Ouchim; the surprisal by the Bashkirs and the advanced posts of the Russian army at Torgau; the private conspiracy at this point against the khan; the long succession of running fights; the parting massacres at the Lake of Tengis under the eyes of the Chinese; and, finally, the tragical retribution to Zebek-Dorchi at the hunting lodge of the Chinese emperor,—all these situations communicate a *scenical* animation tothe wild romance, if treated dramatically; whilst a higher and a philosophic interest belongs to it as a case of authentic history, commemorating a great revolution, for good and for evil, in the fortunes of a whole people,—a people semi-barbarous, but simple hearted, and of ancient descent.

On the 21st of January, 1761, the young Prince Oubacha assumed the sceptre of the Kalmucks upon the death of his father. Some part of the power attached to this dignity he had already wielded since his fourteenth year, in quality of vice-khan, by the express appointment, and with the avowed support, of the Russian government. He was now about eighteen years of age, amiable in his personal character, and not without titles to respect in his public character as a sovereign prince. In times more peaceable, and amongst a people more entirely civilized or more humanized by religion, it is even probable that he might have discharged his high duties with considerable distinction; but his lot was thrown upon stormy times, and a most difficult crisis amongst tribes whose native ferocity was exasperated by debasing forms of superstition, and by a nationality as well as an inflated conceit of their own merit absolutely unparalleled; whilst the circumstances of their hard and trying position under the jealous *surveillance* of an irresistible lord paramount, in the person of the Russian czar, gave a fiercer edge to the natural unamiableness of the Kalmuck disposition, and irritated its gloomier qualities into action under the restless impulses of suspicion and permanent distrust. No prince could hope for a cordial allegiance from his subjects, or a peaceful reignunder the circumstances of the case; for the dilemma in which a Kalmuck ruler stood at present was of this nature: *wanting* the sanction and support of the czar, he was inevitably too weak from without to command confidence from his subjects or resistance to his competitors. On the other hand, *with* this kind of support, and deriving his title in any degree from the favor of the imperial court, he became almost in that extent an object of hatred at home and within the whole compass of his own territory. He was at once an object of hatred for the past, being a living monument of national independence ignominiously surrendered, and an object of jealousy for the future, as one who had already advertised himself to be a fitting tool for the ultimate purposes (whatsoever those might prove to be) of the Russian court. Coming himself to the Kalmuck sceptre under the heaviest weight of prejudice from the unfortunate circumstances of his position, it might have been expected that Oubacha would have been pre-eminently an object of detestation; for, besides his known dependence upon the cabinet of St. Petersburg, the direct line of succession had been set aside, and the principle of inheritance violently suspended, in favor of his own father, so recently as nineteen years before the era of his own accession, consequently within the lively remembrance of the existing generation. He, therefore, almost equally with his father, stood within the full current of the national prejudices, and might have anticipated the most pointed hostility. But it was not so; such are the caprices in human affairs, that he was even, in a moderate sense, popular,—a benefit which wore the more cheering aspect and thepromises of permanence, inasmuch as he owed it exclusively to his personal qualities of kindness and affability, as well as to the beneficence of his government. On the other hand, to balance this unlooked-for prosperity at the outset of his reign, he met with a rival in popular favor—almost a competitor—in the person of Zebek-Dorchi, a prince with considerable pretensions to the throne, and, perhaps it might be said, with equal pretensions. Zebek-Dorchi was a direct descendant of the same royal house as himself, through a different branch. On public grounds his claim stood, perhaps, on a footing equally good with that of Oubacha; whilst his personal qualities, even in those aspects which seemed to a philosophical observer most odious and repulsive, promised the most effectual aid to the dark purposes of an intriguer or a conspirator, and were generally fitted to win a popular support precisely in those points where Oubacha was most defective. He was much superior in external appearance to his rival on the throne, and so far better qualified to win the good opinion of a semi-barbarous people; whilst his dark intellectual qualities of Machiavelian dissimulation, profound hypocrisy, and perfidy which knew no touch of remorse, were admirably calculated to sustain any ground which he might win from the simple-hearted people with whom he had to deal and from the frank carelessness of his unconscious competitor.

At the very outset of his treacherous career Zebek-Dorchi was sagacious enough to perceive that nothing could be gained by open declaration of hostility to the reigning prince. The choice had been a deliberate acton the part of Russia; and Elizabeth Petrowna was not the person to recall her own favors with levity or upon slight grounds. Openly, therefore, to have declared his enmity towards his relative on the throne, could have had no effect but that of arming suspicions against his own ulterior purposes in a quarter where it was most essential to his interest that for the present all suspicion should be hoodwinked. Accordingly, after much meditation, the course he took for opening his snares was this: He raised a rumor that his own life was in danger from the plots of several *saissang* (that is, Kalmuck nobles), who were leagued together under an oath to assassinate him; and immediately after, assuming a well-counterfeited alarm, he fled to Tcherkask, followed by sixty-five tents. From this place he kept up a correspondence with the imperial court; and, by way of soliciting his cause more effectually, he soon repaired in person to St. Petersburg. Once admitted to personal conferences with the cabinet, he found no difficulty in winning over the Russian councils to a concurrence with some of his political views, and thus covertly introducing the point of that wedge which was finally to accomplish his purposes. In particular, he persuaded the Russian government to make a very important alteration in the constitution of the Kalmuck state council, which in effect reorganized the whole political condition of the state and disturbed the balance of power as previously adjusted. Of this council—in the Kalmuck language called *sarga*—there were eight members, called *sargatchi*; and hitherto it had been the custom that these eight members should be entirely subordinate to thekhan; holding, in fact, the ministerial character of secretaries and assistants, but in no respect ranking as co-ordinate authorities. That had produced some inconveniences in former reigns; and it was easy for Zebek-Dorchi to point the jealousy of the Russian court to others more serious which might arise in future circumstances of war or other contingencies. It was resolved, therefore, to place the *sargatchi* henceforward on a footing of perfect independence, and, therefore (as regarded responsibility), on a footing of equality with the khan. Their independence, however, had respect only to their own sovereign; for towards Russia they were placed in a new attitude of direct duty and accountability by the creation in their favor of small pensions (three hundred rubles a year), which, however, to a Kalmuck of that day were more considerable than might be supposed, and had a further value as marks of honorary distinction emanating from a great empress. Thus far the purposes of Zebek-Dorchi were served effectually for the moment; but, apparently, it was only for the moment; since, in the further development of his plots, this very dependency upon Russian influence would be the most serious obstacle in his way. There was, however, another point carried, which outweighed all inferior considerations, as it gave him a power of setting aside discretionally whatsoever should arise to disturb his plots,—he was himself appointed president and controller of the *sargatchi*. The Russian court had been aware of his high pretensions by birth, and hoped by this promotion to satisfy the ambition which, in some degree, was acknowledged to be a reasonable passion for any man occupying his situation.

Having thus completely blindfolded the cabinet of Russia, Zebek-Dorchi proceeded in his new character to fulfil his political mission with the Khan of the Kalmucks. So artfully did he prepare the road for his favorable reception at the court of this prince, that he was at once and universally welcomed as a public benefactor. The pensions of the councillors were so much additional wealth poured into the Tartar exchequer: as to the ties of dependency thus created, experience had not yet enlightened these simple tribes as to that result. And that he himself should be the chief of these mercenary councillors, was so far from being charged upon Zebek as any offence or any ground of suspicion, that his relative the khan returned him hearty thanks for his services, under the belief that he could have accepted this appointment only with a view to keep out other and more unwelcome pretenders, who would not have had the same motives of consanguinity or friendship for executing its duties in a spirit of kindness to the Kalmucks. The first use which he made of his new functions about the khan's person was to attack the court of Russia, by a romantic villany not easily to be credited, for those very acts of interference with the council which he himself had prompted. This was a dangerous step; but it was indispensable to his further advance upon the gloomy path which he had traced out for himself. A triple vengeance was what he meditated: 1. Upon the Russian cabinet, for having undervalued his own pretensions to the throne; 2. Upon his amiable rival, for having supplanted him; and, 3. Upon all those of the nobility who had manifested their sense of his weakness by their neglect, or their sense of his perfidious character by their suspicions. Here was a colossal outline of wickedness; and by one in his situation, feeble (as it might seem) for the accomplishment of its humblest parts, how was the total edifice to be reared in its comprehensive grandeur? He, a worm as he was,—could he venture to assail the mighty behemoth of Muscovy, the potentate who counted three hundred languages around the footsteps of his

throne, and from whose "lion ramp" recoiled alike "baptized and infidel,"—
Christendom on the one side, strong by her intellect and her organization,
and the "barbaric East" on the other, with her unnumbered numbers? The
match was a monstrous one; but in its very monstrosity there lay this germ
of encouragement,—that it could not be suspected. The very hopelessness
of the scheme grounded his hope; and he resolved to execute a vengeance
which should involve as it were, in the unity of a well-laid tragic fable, all of
whom he judged to be his enemies. That vengeance lay in detaching from
the Russian empire the whole Kalmuck nation and breaking up that system
of intercourse which had thus far been beneficial to both. This last was a
consideration which moved him but little. True it was that Russia to the
Kalmucks had secured lands and extensive pasturage; true it was that the
Kalmucks reciprocally to Russia had furnished a powerful cavalry; but the
latter loss would be part of his triumph, and the former might be more than
compensated in other climates, under other sovereigns. Here was a scheme
which, in its final accomplishment, would avenge him bitterly on the
czarina, and in the course of its accomplishment might furnish him with
ample occasions forremoving his other enemies. It may be readily
supposed, indeed, that he who could deliberately raise his eyes to the
Russian autocrat as an antagonist in single duel with himself was not likely
to feel much anxiety about Kalmuck enemies of whatever rank. He took his
resolution, therefore, sternly and irrevocably to effect this astonishing
translation of an ancient people across the pathless deserts of Central Asia,
intersected continually by rapid rivers rarely furnished with bridges, and of
which the fords were known only to those who might think it for their
interest to conceal them, through many nations inhospitable or hostile,—
frost and snow around them (from the necessity of commencing their flight
in the winter), famine in their front, and the sabre, or even the artillery, of
an offended and mighty empress hanging upon their rear for thousands of
miles. But what was to be their final mark, the port of shelter, after so
fearful a course of wandering? Two things were evident: it must be some
power at a great distance from Russia, so as to make return even in that
view hopeless, and it must be a power of sufficient rank to insure them
protection from any hostile efforts on the part of the czarina for reclaiming
them or for chastising their revolt. Both conditions were united obviously
in the person of Kien Long, the reigning emperor of China, who was
further recommended to them by his respect for the head of their religion.
To China, therefore, and, as their first rendezvous, to the shadow of the
great Chinese Wall, it was settled by Zebek that they should direct their
flight.

Next came the question of time, *When* should the flight commence? and,
finally, the more delicate question as tothe choice of accomplices. To
extend the knowledge of the conspiracy too far was to insure its betrayal to

the Russian government. Yet at some stage of the preparations it was evident that a very extensive confidence must be made, because in no other way could the mass of the Kalmuck population be persuaded to furnish their families with the requisite equipments for so long a migration. This critical step, however, it was resolved to defer up to the latest possible moment, and, at all events, to make no general communication on the subject until the time of departure should be definitely settled. In the mean time Zebek admitted only three persons to his confidence,—of whom Oubacha, the reigning prince, was almost necessarily one; but him, from his yielding and somewhat feeble character, he viewed rather in the light of a tool than as one of his active accomplices. Those whom (if anybody) he admitted to an unreserved participation in his counsels were two only,—the great *lama* among the Kalmucks, and his own father-in-law, Erempel, a ruling prince of some tribe in the neighborhood of the Caspian Sea, recommended to his favor not so much by any strength of talent corresponding to the occasion, as by his blind devotion to himself and his passionate anxiety to promote the elevation of his daughter and his son-in-law to the throne of a sovereign prince. A titular prince Zebek already was; but this dignity, without the substantial accompaniment of a sceptre, seemed but an empty sound to both of these ambitious rivals. The other accomplice, whose name was Loosang-Dchaltzan, and whose rank was that of lama, or Kalmuck pontiff, was a person of far more distinguished pretensions. Hehad something of the same gloomy and terrific pride which marked the character of Zebek himself, manifesting also the same energy, accompanied by the same unfaltering cruelty, and a natural facility of dissimulation even more profound. It was by this man that the other question was settled as to the time for giving effect to their designs. His own pontifical character had suggested to him, that in order to strengthen their influence with the vast mob of simple-minded men whom they were to lead into a howling wilderness, after persuading them to lay desolate their own ancient hearths, it was indispensable that they should be able, in cases of extremity, to plead the express sanction of God for their entire enterprise. This could only be done by addressing themselves to the great head of their religion,—the dalai lama of Tibet. Him they easily persuaded to countenance their schemes; and an oracle was delivered solemnly at Tibet, to the effect that no ultimate prosperity would attend this great exodus unless it were pursued through the years of the *tiger* and the *hare*. Now, the Kalmuck custom is to distinguish their years by attaching to each a denomination taken from one of twelve animals, the exact order of succession being absolutely fixed; so that the cycle revolves, of course, through a period of a dozen years. Consequently, if the approaching year of the *tiger* were suffered to escape them, in that case the expedition must be delayed for twelve years more; within which period, even were no other unfavorable changes to arise, it was pretty well foreseen that the Russian government would take the most effectual means for bridling their vagrant propensities by a ring fence of forts, or military posts, tosay nothing of the still readier plan for securing their fidelity (a plan already talked of in all quarters) by exacting a large body of hostages selected from the families of the most influential nobles. On these cogent considerations, it was solemnly determined that this terrific experiment should be made in the next year of the *tiger*, which happened to fall upon the Christian year 1771. With respect to the month, there was, unhappily for the Kalmucks, even less latitude allowed to their choice than with respect to the year. It was absolutely necessary, or it was thought so, that the different divisions of the nation, which pastured their flocks on both banks of the Wolga, should have the means of effecting an instantaneous junction, because the danger of being intercepted by flying columns of the imperial armies was precisely the greatest at the outset. Now, from the want of bridges or sufficient river craft for transporting so vast a body of men, the sole means which could be depended upon (especially where so many women, children, and camels were concerned) was *ice*; and this, in a state of sufficient firmness, could not be absolutely counted upon before the month of January. Hence it happened that this astonishing exodus of a whole nation, before so much as a whisper of the design had begun to circulate amongst those whom it most interested, before it was even suspected that any man's wishes pointed in that direction, had been definitively appointed for January of the year 1771; and, almost up to the Christmas of 1770, the poor, simple Kalmuck herdsmen and their families were going nightly to their peaceful beds without even dreaming that the *fiat* had already gone forth from theirrulers which consigned those quiet abodes, together with the peace and comfort which reigned within them, to a withering desolation, now close at hand.

Meantime war raged on a great scale between Russia and the sultan; and, until the time arrived for throwing off their vassalage, it was necessary that Oubacha should contribute his usual contingent of martial aid; nay, it had unfortunately become prudent that he should contribute much more than his usual aid. Human experience gives ample evidence that in some mysterious and unaccountable way no great design is ever agitated, no matter how few or how faithful may be the participators, but that some presentiment—some dim misgiving—is kindled amongst those whom it is chiefly important to blind. And, however it might have happened, certain it is that already, when as yet no syllable of the conspiracy had been breathed to any man whose very existence was not staked upon its concealment, nevertheless some vague and uneasy jealousy had arisen in the Russian cabinet as to the future schemes of the Kalmuck khan; and very probable it is that, but for the war then raging, and the consequent prudence of conciliating a very important vassal, or, at least, of abstaining from what would powerfully alienate him, even at that moment such measures would have been adopted as must forever have intercepted the Kalmuck schemes. Slight as were the jealousies of the imperial court, they had not escaped the Machiavelian eyes of Zebek and the lama; and under their guidance, Oubacha, bending to the circumstances of the moment, and meeting the jealousy of the Russian court with a policy corresponding to their own, strove by unusualzeal to efface the czarina's unfavorable impressions. He enlarged the scale of his contributions, and *that* so prodigiously, that he absolutely carried to head-quarters a force of thirty-five thousand cavalry, fully equipped. Some go further, and rate the amount beyond forty thousand; but the smaller estimate is, at all events, *within* the truth.

With this magnificent array of cavalry, heavy as well as light, the khan went into the field under great expectations; and these he more than realized. Having the good fortune to be concerned with so ill-organized and disorderly a description of force as that which at all times composed the bulk of a Turkish army, he carried victory along with his banners; gained many partial successes; and, at last, in a pitched battle, overthrew the Turkish force opposed to him, with a loss of five thousand men left upon the field.

These splendid achievements seemed likely to operate in various ways against the impending revolt. Oubacha had now a strong motive, in the martial glory acquired, for continuing his connection with the empire in whose service he had won it and by whom only it could be fully appreciated. He was now a great marshal of a great empire,—one of the Paladins around the imperial throne. In China he would be nobody, or (worse than that) a mendicant alien, prostrate at the feet, and soliciting the precarious alms, of a prince with whom he had no connection. Besides, it might reasonably be expected that the czarina, grateful for the really efficient aid given by the Tartar prince, would confer upon him such eminent rewards as might be sufficient to anchor his hopes uponRussia and to wean him from every possible seduction. These were the obvious suggestions of prudence and good sense to every man who stood neutral in the case. But they were disappointed. The czarina knew her obligations to the khan; but she did not acknowledge them. Wherefore? That is a mystery perhaps never to be explained. So it was, however. The khan went unhonored; no *ukase* ever proclaimed his merits; and, perhaps, had he even been abundantly recompensed by Russia, there were others who would have defeated these tendencies to reconciliation. Erempel, Zebek, and Loosang the lama were pledged life-deep to prevent any accommodation; and their efforts were unfortunately seconded by those of their deadliest enemies. In the Russian court there were at that time some great nobles preoccupied with feelings of hatred and blind malice towards the

Kalmucks, quite as strong as any which the Kalmucks could harbor towards Russia, and not, perhaps, so well founded. Just as much as the Kalmucks hated the Russian yoke, their galling assumption of authority, the marked air of disdain, as towards a nation of ugly, stupid, and filthy barbarians, which too generally marked the Russian bearing and language,—but, above all, the insolent contempt, or even outrages, which the Russian governors or great military commandants tolerated in their followers towards the barbarous religion and superstitious mummeries of the Kalmuck priesthood,—precisely in that extent did the ferocity of the Russian resentment, and their wrath at seeing the trampled worm turn or attempt a feeble retaliation, react upon the unfortunate Kalmucks. At this crisis it is probable thatenvy and wounded pride, upon witnessing the splendid victories of Oubacha and Momotbacha over the Turks and Bashkirs, contributed strength to the Russian irritation; and it must have been through the intrigues of those nobles about her person who chiefly smarted under these feelings that the czarina could ever have lent herself to the unwise and ungrateful policy pursued at this critical period towards the Kalmuck khan. That czarina was no longer Elizabeth Petrowna; it was Catharine the Second,—a princess who did not often err so injuriously (injuriously for herself as much as for others) in the measures of her government. She had soon ample reason for repenting of her false policy. Meantime, how much it must have co-operated with the other motives previously acting upon Oubacha in sustaining his determination to revolt, and how powerfully it must have assisted the efforts of all the Tartar chieftains in preparing the minds of their people to feel the necessity of this difficult enterprise, by arming their pride and their suspicions against the Russian government, through the keenness of their sympathy with the wrongs of their insulted prince, may be readily imagined. It is a fact, and it has been confessed by candid Russians themselves when treating of this great dismemberment, that the conduct of the Russian cabinet throughout the period of suspense, and during the crisis of hesitation in the Kalmuck council, was exactly such as was most desirable for the purposes of the conspirators; it was such, in fact, as to set the seal to all their machinations, by supplying distinct evidences and official vouchers for what could otherwise have been, at the most, matters of doubtful suspicion and indirect presumption.

Nevertheless, in the face of all these arguments, and even allowing their weight so far as not at all to deny the injustice or the impolicy of the imperial ministers, it is contended by many persons who have reviewed the affair with a command of all the documents bearing on the case, more especially the letters or minutes of council subsequently discovered, in the handwriting of Zebek-Dorchi, and the important evidence of the Russian captive Weseloff, who was carried off by the Kalmucks in their flight, that beyond all doubt Oubacha was powerless for any purpose of impeding, or even of delaying the revolt. He himself, indeed, was under religious obligations of the most terrific solemnity never to flinch from the enterprise or even to slacken in his zeal; for Zebek-Dorchi, distrusting the firmness of his resolution under any unusual pressure of alarm or difficulty, had, in the very earliest stage of the conspiracy, availed himself of the khan's well-known superstition, to engage him, by means of previous concert with the priests and their head the lama, in some dark and mysterious rites of consecration, terminating in oaths under such terrific sanctions as no Kalmuck would have courage to violate. As far, therefore, as regarded the personal share of the khan in what was to come, Zebek was entirely at his ease. He knew him to be so deeply pledged by religious terrors to the prosecution of the conspiracy, that no honors within the czarina's gift could have possibly shaken his adhesion; and then, as to threats from the same quarter, he knew him to be sealed against those fears by others of a gloomier character and better adapted to his peculiar temperament. For Oubacha was a brave man, as respected allbodily enemies or the dangers of human warfare, but was as sensitive and timid as the most superstitious of old women in facing the frowns of a priest or under the vague anticipations of ghostly retributions. But had it been otherwise, and had there been any reason to apprehend an unsteady demeanor on the part of this prince at the approach of the critical moment, such were the changes already effected in the state of their domestic politics amongst the Tartars by the undermining arts of Zebek-Dorchi, and his ally the lama, that very little importance would have attached to that doubt. All power was now effectually lodged in the hands of Zebek-Dorchi. He was the true and absolute wielder of the Kalmuck sceptre. All measures of importance were submitted to his discretion, and nothing was finally resolved but under his dictation. This result he had brought about in a year or two by means sufficiently simple: first of all, by availing himself of the prejudice in his favor, so largely diffused amongst the lowest of the Kalmucks, that his own title to the throne, in quality of great-grandson in a direct line from Ajouka, the most illustrious of all the Kalmuck khans, stood upon a better basis than that of Oubacha, who derived from a collateral branch; secondly, with respect to that sole advantage which Oubacha possessed above himself in the ratification of his title, by improving this difference between their situations to the disadvantage of his competitor, as one who had not scrupled to accept that triumph from an alien power at the price of his independence, which he himself (as he would have it understood) disdained to court; thirdly, by his own talents and address, coupled with the ferocious energy of his moral character; fourthly,—and perhaps in an equal degree,—by the criminal facility and good-nature of Oubacha; finally (which is remarkable enough, as illustrating the character of the man), by that very new modelling of the *sarga*, or privy council, which he had used as a principal topic of abuse and malicious insinuation against the Russian government, whilst in reality he first had suggested the alteration to the empress, and he chiefly appropriated the political advantages which it was fitted to yield. For, as he was himself appointed the chief of the *sargatchi*, and as the pensions of the inferior *sargatchi* passed through his hands, whilst in effect they owed their appointments to his nomination, it may be easily supposed that whatever power existed in the state capable of controlling the khan, being held by the *sarga* under its new organization, and this body being completely under his influence, the final result was to throw all the functions of the state, whether nominally in the prince or in the council, substantially into the hands of this one man; whilst at the same time, from the strict league which he maintained with the lama, all the thunders of the spiritual power were always ready to come in aid of the magistrate or to supply his incapacity in cases which he could not reach.

But the time was now rapidly approaching for the mighty experiment. The day was drawing near on which the signal was to be given for raising the standard of revolt, and, by a combined movement on both sides of the Wolga, for spreading the smoke of one vast conflagration that should wrap in a common blaze their own huts and the stately cities of their enemies over thebreadth and length of those great provinces in which their flocks were dispersed. The year of the *tiger* was now within one little month of its commencement. The fifth morning of that year was fixed for the fatal day when the fortunes and happiness of a whole nation were to be put upon the hazard of a dicer's throw; and, as yet, that nation was in profound ignorance of the whole plan. The khan, such was the kindness of his nature, could not bring himself to make the revelation so urgently required. It was clear, however, that this could not be delayed; and Zebek-Dorchi took the task willingly upon himself. But where or how should this notification be made, so as to exclude Russian hearers? After some deliberation, the following plan was adopted: Couriers, it was contrived, should arrive in furious haste, one upon the heels of another, reporting a sudden inroad of the Kirghises and Bashkirs upon the Kalmuck lands at a point distant about one hundred and twenty miles. Thither all the Kalmuck families, according to immemorial custom, were required to send a separate representative; and there, accordingly, within three days, all appeared. The distance, the solitary ground appointed for the rendezvous, the rapidity of the march, all tended to make it almost certain that no Russian could be present. Zebek-Dorchi then came forward. He did not waste many words upon rhetoric. He unfurled an immense sheet of parchment, visible from the outermost distance at which any of this vast crowd could stand. The total number amounted to eighty thousand: all saw, and many heard. They were told of the oppressions of Russia; of her pride and haughty disdain, evidencedtowards them by a thousand acts; of her contempt for their religion; of her determination to reduce them to absolute slavery; of the preliminary measures she had already taken by erecting forts upon many of the great rivers of their neighborhood; of the ulterior intentions she thus announced to circumscribe their pastoral lands, until they would all be obliged to renounce their flocks, and to collect in towns like Sarepta, there to pursue mechanical and servile trades of shoemaker, tailor, and weaver, such as the freeborn Tartar had always disdained. "Then, again," said the subtle prince, "she increases her military levies upon our population every year. We pour out our blood as young men in her defence, or more often in support of her insolent aggressions; and, as old men, we reap nothing from our sufferings nor benefit by our survivorship where so many are sacrificed." At this point of his harangue Zebek produced several papers (forged, as it is generally believed, by himself and the lama), containing projects of the Russian court for a general transfer of the eldest sons, taken *en masse* from the greatest Kalmuck families, to the imperial court. "Now, let this be once accomplished," he argued, "and there is an end of all useful resistance from that day forwards. Petitions we might make, or even remonstrances; as men of words, we might play a bold part; but for deeds, for that sort of language by which our ancestors were used to speak, holding us by such a chain, Russia would make a jest of our wishes, knowing full well that we should not dare to make any effectual movement."

Having thus sufficiently roused the angry passions of his vast audience, and having alarmed their fears by thispretended scheme against their first-born (an artifice which was indispensable to his purpose, because it met beforehand *every* form of amendment to his proposal coming from the more moderate nobles, who would not otherwise have failed to insist upon trying the effect of bold addresses to the empress before resorting to any desperate extremity), Zebek-Dorchi opened his scheme of revolt, and, if so, of instant revolt: since any preparations reported at St. Petersburg would be a signal for the armies of Russia to cross into such positions from all parts of Asia as would effectually intercept their march. It is remarkable, however, that, with all his audacity and his reliance upon the momentary excitement of the Kalmucks, the subtle prince did not venture at this stage of his seduction to make so startling a proposal as that of a flight to China. All that he held out for the present was a rapid march to the Temba or some other great river, which they were to cross, and to take up a strong position on the farther bank, from which, as from a post of conscious security, they could hold a bolder language to the czarina, and one which would have a better chance of winning a favorable audience.

These things, in the irritated condition of the simple Tartars, passed by acclamation; and all returned homewards to push forward with the most furious speed the preparations for their awful undertaking. Rapid and energetic these of necessity were; and in that degree they became noticeable and manifest to the Russians who happened to be intermingled with the different hordes, either on commercial errands or as agents officially from the Russian government,—some in a financial, others in a diplomatic character.

Amongst these last (indeed, at the head of them) was a Russian of some distinction, by name Kichinskoi,—a man memorable for his vanity, and memorable also as one of the many victims to the Tartar revolution. This Kichinskoi had been sent by the empress as her envoy to overlook the conduct of the Kalmucks. He was styled the *grand pristaw*, or great commissioner, and was universally known amongst the Tartar tribes by this title. His mixed character of ambassador and of political *surveillant*, combined with the dependent state of the Kalmucks, gave him a real weight in the Tartar councils, and might have given him a far greater had not his outrageous self-conceit and his arrogant confidence in his own authority, as due chiefly to his personal qualities for command, led him into such harsh displays of power and menaces so odious to the Tartar pride as very soon made him an object of their profoundest malice. He had publicly insulted the khan; and upon making a communication to him to the effect that some reports began to circulate, and even to reach the empress, of a design in agitation to fly from the imperial dominions, he had ventured to say, "But this you dare not attempt. I laugh at such rumors; yes, khan, I laugh at them to the empress; for you are a chained bear, and that you know." The khan turned away on his heel with marked disdain; and the pristaw, foaming at the mouth, continued to utter, amongst those of the khan's attendants who stayed behind to catch his real sentiments in a moment of unguarded passion, all that the blindest frenzy of rage could suggest to the most presumptuous of fools. It was now ascertained that suspicions *had* arisen; but at the same time it was ascertainedthat the pristaw spoke no more than the truth in representing himself to have discredited these suspicions. The fact was, that the mere infatuation of vanity made him believe that nothing could go on undetected by his all-piercing sagacity, and that no rebellion could prosper when rebuked by his commanding presence. The Tartars, therefore, pursued their preparations, confiding in the obstinate blindness of the grand pristaw, as in their perfect safeguard. And such it proved, to his own ruin as well as that of myriads beside.

Christmas arrived; and a little before that time courier upon courier came dropping in, one upon the very heels of another, to St. Petersburg, assuring the czarina that beyond all doubt the Kalmucks were in the very crisis of departure. These despatches came from the governor of Astrachan, and copies were instantly forwarded to Kichinskoi. Now, it happened that between this governor—a Russian named Beketoff—and the pristaw had been an ancient feud. The very name of Beketoff inflamed his resentment; and no sooner did he see that hated name attached to the despatch than he felt himself confirmed in his former views with tenfold bigotry, and wrote instantly, in terms of the most pointed ridicule, against the new alarmist, pledging his own head upon the visionariness of his alarms. Beketoff, however, was not to be put down by a few hard words or by ridicule. He persisted in his statements. The Russian ministry were confounded by the obstinacy of the disputants; and some were beginning even to treat the governor of Astrachan as a bore and as the dupe of his own nervous terrors, when the memorable day arrived, thefatal 5th of January, which forever terminated the dispute and put a seal upon the earthly hopes and fortunes of unnumbered myriads. The governor of Astrachan was the first to hear the news. Stung by the mixed furies of jealousy, of triumphant vengeance, and of anxious ambition, he sprang into his sledge, and, at the rate of three hundred miles a day, pursued his route to St. Petersburg, rushed into the imperial presence, announced the total realization of his worst predictions, and upon the confirmation of this intelligence by subsequent despatches from many different posts on the Wolga, he received an imperial commission to seize the person of his deluded enemy and to keep him in strict captivity. These orders were eagerly fulfilled; and the unfortunate Kichinskoi soon afterwards expired of grief and mortification in the gloomy solitude of a dungeon,—a victim to his own immeasurable vanity and the blinding self-delusions of a presumption that refused all warning.

The governor of Astrachan had been but too faithful a prophet. Perhaps even *he* was surprised at the suddenness with which the verification followed his reports. Precisely on the 5th of January, the day so solemnly appointed under religious sanctions by the lama, the Kalmucks on the east bank of the Wolga were seen at the earliest dawn of day assembling by troops and squadrons and in the tumultuous movement of some great morning of battle. Tens of thousands continued moving off the ground at every half-hour's interval. Women and children, to the amount of two hundred thousand and upwards, were placed upon wagons or upon camels and drew off by masses of twenty thousand at once, placed under suitableescorts, and continually swelled in numbers by other outlying bodies of the horde who kept falling in at various distances upon the first and second day's march. From sixty to eighty thousand of those who were the best mounted stayed behind the rest of the tribes, with purposes of devastation and plunder more violent than prudence justified or the amiable character of the khan could be supposed to approve. But in this, as in other instances, he was completely overruled by the malignant counsels of Zebek-Dorchi. The first tempest of the desolating fury of the Tartars discharged itself upon their own habitations. But this, as cutting off all infirm looking backward from the hardships of their march, had been thought so necessary a measure by all the chieftains that even Oubacha himself was the first to authorize the act by his own example. He seized a torch, previously prepared with materials the most durable as well as combustible, and steadily applied it to the timbers of his own palace. Nothing was saved from the general wreck except the portable part of the domestic utensils and that part of the woodwork which could be applied to the manufacture of the long Tartar lances. This chapter in their memorable day's work being finished, and the whole of their villages throughout a district of ten thousand square miles in one simultaneous blaze, the Tartars waited for further orders.

These, it was intended, should have taken a character of valedictory vengeance, and thus have left behind to the czarina a dreadful commentary upon the main motives of their flight. It was the purpose of Zebek-Dorchi that all the Russian towns, churches, and buildings of every description should be given up to pillage and destruction, and such treatment applied to the defenceless inhabitants as might naturally be expected from a fierce people already infuriated by the spectacle of their own outrages and by the bloody retaliations which they must necessarily have provoked. This part of the tragedy, however, was happily intercepted by a providential disappointment at the very crisis of departure. It has been mentioned already that the motive for selecting the depth of winter as the season of flight (which otherwise was obviously the very worst possible) had been the impossibility of effecting a junction sufficiently rapid with the tribes on the west of the Wolga, in the absence of bridges, unless by a natural bridge of ice. For this one advantage the Kalmuck leaders had consented to aggravate by a thousand-fold the calamities inevitable to a rapid flight over boundless tracts of country with women, children, and herds of cattle,—for this one single advantage; and yet, after all, it was lost. The reason never has been explained satisfactorily; but the fact was such. Some have said that the signals were not properly concerted for marking the moment of absolute departure; that is, for signifying whether the settled intention of the eastern Kalmucks might not have been suddenly interrupted by adverse intelligence. Others have supposed that the ice might not be equally strong on both sides of the river, and might even be generally insecure for the treading of heavy and heavily laden animals such as camels. But the prevailing notion is, that some accidental movements on the 3rd and 4th of January of Russian troops in the neighborhood of the western Kalmucks, though really having no reference to them or their plans, had been construed into certain signs that all was discovered, and that the prudence of the western chieftains, who, from situation, had never been exposed to those intrigues which Zebek-Dorchi had practised upon the pride of the eastern tribes, now stepped in to save their people from ruin. Be the cause what it might, it is certain that the western Kalmucks were in some way prevented from forming the intended junction with their brethren of the opposite bank; and the result was, that at least one hundred thousand of these Tartars were left behind in Russia. This accident it was which saved their Russian neighbors universally from the desolation which else awaited them. One general massacre and conflagration would assuredly have surprised them, to the utter extermination of their property, their houses, and themselves, had it not been for this disappointment. But the eastern chieftains did not dare to put to hazard the safety of their brethren under the first impulse of the czarina's vengeance for so dreadful a tragedy; for, as they were well aware of too many circumstances by which she might discover the concurrence of the western people in the general scheme of revolt, they justly feared that she would thence infer their concurrence also in the bloody events which marked its outset.

Little did the western Kalmucks guess what reasons they also had for gratitude on account of an interposition so unexpected, and which, at the moment, they so generally deplored. Could they but have witnessed the thousandth part of the sufferings which overtook their eastern brethren in the first month of their sad flight,they would have blessed Heaven for their own narrow escape; and yet these sufferings of the first month were but a prelude or foretaste comparatively slight of those which afterwards succeeded.

For now began to unroll the most awful series of calamities and the most extensive which is anywhere recorded to have visited the sons and daughters of men. It is possible that the sudden inroads of destroying nations, such as the Huns, or the Avars, or the Mongol Tartars, may have inflicted misery as extensive; but there the misery and the desolation would be sudden, like the flight of volleying lightning. Those who were spared at first would generally be spared to the end; those who perished would perish instantly. It is possible that the French retreat from Moscow may have made some nearer approach to this calamity in duration, though still a feeble and miniature approach; for the French sufferings did not commence in good earnest until about one month from the time of leaving Moscow; and though it is true that afterwards the vials of wrath were emptied upon the devoted army for six or seven weeks in succession, yet what is that to this Kalmuck tragedy, which lasted for more than as many months? But the main feature of horror, by which the Tartar march was distinguished from the French, lies in the accompaniment of women and children. There were both, it is true, with the French army, but so few as to bear no visible proportion to the total numbers concerned. The French, in short, were merely an army,—a host of professional destroyers, whose regular trade was bloodshed and whose regular element was danger and suffering; but the Tartars were a nation carrying along with them more than two hundred and fifty thousand women and children, utterly unequal, for the most part, to any contest with the calamities before them. The children of Israel were in the same circumstances as to the accompaniment of their families; but they were released from the pursuit of their enemies in a very early stage of their flight; and their subsequent residence in the desert was not a march, but a continued halt, and under a continued interposition of Heaven for their comfortable support. Earthquakes, again, however comprehensive in their ravages, are shocks of a moment's duration. A much nearer approach made to the wide range and the long duration of the Kalmuck tragedy may have been in a pestilence such as that which visited Athens in the Peloponnesian war or London in the reign of Charles II. There, also, the martyrs were counted by myriads, and the period of the desolation was counted by months. But, after all, the total amount of destruction was on a smaller scale; and there was this feature of alleviation to the *conscious* pressure of the calamity,—that the misery was withdrawn from public notice into private chambers and hospitals. The siege of Jerusalem by Vespasian and his son, taken in its entire circumstances, comes nearest of all for breadth and depth of suffering, for duration, for the exasperation of the suffering from without by internal feuds, and, finally, for that last most appalling expression of the furnace heat of the anguish in its power to extinguish the natural affections even of maternal love. But, after all, each case had circumstances of romantic misery peculiar to itself,—circumstances without precedent, and (wherever human nature is ennobled by Christianity) it may be confidently hoped never to be repeated.

The first point to be reached, before any hope of repose could be encouraged, was the river Jaik. This was not above three hundred miles from the main point of departure on the Wolga; and, if the march thither was to be a forced one and a severe one, it was alleged, on the other hand, that the suffering would be the more brief and transient; one summary exertion, not to be repeated, and all was achieved. Forced the march was, and severe beyond example,—there the forewarning proved correct; but the promised rest proved a mere phantom of the wilderness,—a visionary rainbow, which fled before their hopesick eyes, across these interminable solitudes, for seven months of hardship and calamity, without a pause. These sufferings, by their very nature and the circumstances under which they arose, were (like the scenery of the *steppes*) somewhat monotonous in their coloring and external features: what variety, however, there was will be most naturally exhibited by tracing historically the successive stages of the general misery exactly as it unfolded itself under the double agency of weakness still increasing from within and hostile pressure from without. Viewed in this manner, under the real order of development, it is remarkable that these sufferings of the Tartars, though under the moulding hands of accident, arrange themselves almost with a scenical propriety. They seem combined as with the skill of an artist, the intensity of the misery advancing regularly with the advances of the march, and the stages of the calamity corresponding to the stages of the route; so that, uponraising the curtain which veils the great catastrophe, we behold one vast climax of anguish, towering upwards by regular gradations as if constructed artificially for picturesque effect,—a result which might not have been surprising had it been reasonable to anticipate the same rate of speed, and even an accelerated rate, as prevailing through the later stages of the expedition. But it seemed, on the contrary, most reasonable to calculate upon a continual decrement in the rate of motion according to the increasing distance from the head-quarters of the pursuing enemy. This calculation, however, was defeated by the extraordinary circumstance that the Russian armies did not begin to close in very fiercely upon the Kalmucks until after they had accomplished a distance of full two thousand miles. One thousand miles farther on the assaults became even more tumultuous and murderous; and already the great shadows of the Chinese Wall were dimly descried, when the frenzy and *acharnement* of the pursuers and the bloody desperation of the miserable fugitives had reached its uttermost extremity. Let us briefly rehearse the main stages of the misery and trace the ascending steps of the tragedy according to the great divisions of the route marked out by the central rivers of Asia.

The first stage, we have already said, was from the Wolga to the Jaik; the distance about three hundred miles; the time allowed seven days. For the first week, therefore, the rate of marching averaged about forty-three English miles a day. The weather was cold, but bracing; and, at a more moderate pace, this part of the journey might have been accomplished without muchdistress by a people as hardy as the Kalmucks. As it was, the cattle suffered greatly from over-driving; milk began to fail even for the children; the sheep perished by wholesale; and the children themselves were saved only by the innumerable camels.

The Cossacks who dwelt upon the banks of the Jaik were the first among the subjects of Russia to come into collision with the Kalmucks. Great was their surprise at the suddenness of the irruption, and great also their consternation; for, according to their settled custom, by far the greater part of their number was absent during the winter months at the fisheries upon the Caspian. Some who were liable to surprise at the most exposed points fled in crowds to the fortress of Koulagina, which was immediately invested and summoned by Oubacha. He had, however, in his train only a few light pieces of artillery; and the Russian commandant at Koulagina, being aware of the hurried circumstances in which the khan was placed, and that he stood upon the very edge, as it were, of a renewed flight, felt encouraged by these considerations to a more obstinate resistance than might else have been advisable with an enemy so little disposed to observe the usages of civilized warfare. The period of his anxiety was not long. On the fifth day of the siege he descried from the walls a succession of Tartar couriers, mounted upon fleet Bactrian camels, crossing the vast plains around the fortress at a furious pace and riding into the Kalmuck encampment at various points. Great agitation appeared immediately to follow. Orders were soon after despatched in all directions; and it became speedily known that upon a distant flank of the Kalmuck movement a bloody and exterminating battle had been fought the day before, in which one entire tribe of the khan's dependants, numbering not less than nine thousand fighting men, had perished to the last man. This was the *ouloss*, or clan, called *Feka-Zechorr*, between whom and the Cossacks there was a feud of ancient standing. In selecting, therefore, the points of attack, on occasion of the present hasty inroad, the Cossack chiefs were naturally eager so to direct their efforts as to combine with the service of the empress some gratification to their own party hatreds, more especially as the present was likely to be their final opportunity for revenge if the Kalmuck evasion should prosper. Having, therefore, concentrated as large a body of Cossack cavalry as circumstances allowed, they attacked the hostile *ouloss* with a precipitation which denied to it all means for communicating with Oubacha; for the necessity of commanding an ample range of pasturage, to meet the necessities of their vast flocks and herds, had separated this *ouloss* from the khan's head-quarters by an interval of eighty miles: and thus it was, and not from oversight, that it came to be thrown entirely upon its own resources. These had proved insufficient. Retreat, from the exhausted state of their horses and camels, no less than from the prodigious encumbrances of their live stock, was absolutely out of the question. Quarter was disdained on the one side, and would not have been granted on the other; and thus it had happened that the setting sun of that one day (the thirteenth from the first opening of the revolt) threw his parting rays upon the final agonies of an ancient *ouloss*, stretched upon a bloody field, who on that day's dawning had held and styled themselves an independent nation.

Universal consternation was diffused through the wide borders of the khan's encampment by this disastrous intelligence, not so much on account of the numbers slain, or the total extinction of a powerful ally, as because the position of the Cossack force was likely to put to hazard the future advances of the Kalmucks, or at least to retard and hold them in check until the heavier columns of the Russian army should arrive upon their flanks.

The siege of Koulagina was instantly raised; and that signal, so fatal to the happiness of the women and their children, once again resounded through the tents,—the signal for flight, and this time for a flight more rapid than ever. About one hundred and fifty miles ahead of their present position there arose a tract of hilly country, forming a sort of margin to the vast, sealike expanse of champaign savannas, steppes, and occasionally of sandy deserts, which stretched away on each side of this margin both eastwards and westwards. Pretty nearly in the centre of this hilly range lay a narrow defile, through which passed the nearest and the most practicable route to the river Torgai (the farther bank of which river offered the next great station of security for a general halt). It was the more essential to gain this pass before the Cossacks, inasmuch as not only would the delay in forcing the pass give time to the Russian pursuing columns for combining their attacks and for bringing up their artillery, but also because (even if all enemies in pursuit were thrown out of the question) it was held, by those best acquainted with the difficult and obscure geography of these pathless steppes, that theloss of this one narrow strait amongst the hills would have the effect of throwing them (as their only alternative in a case where so wide a sweep of pasturage was required) upon a circuit of at least five hundred miles extra; besides that, after all, this circuitous route would carry them to the Torgai at a point ill fitted for the passage of their heavy baggage. The defile in the hills, therefore, it was resolved to gain; and yet, unless they moved upon it with the velocity of light cavalry, there was little chance but it would be found preoccupied by the Cossacks. They, it is true, had suffered greatly in the recent sanguinary action with their enemies; but the excitement of victory, and the intense sympathy with their unexampled triumph, had again swelled their ranks, and would probably act with the force of a vortex to draw in their simple countrymen from the Caspian. The question, therefore, of preoccupation was reduced to a race. The Cossacks were marching upon an oblique line not above fifty miles longer than that which led to the same point from the Kalmuck head-quarters before Koulagina; and therefore, without the most furious haste on the part of the Kalmucks, there was not a chance for them, burdened and "trashed" as they were, to anticipate so agile a light cavalry as the Cossacks in seizing this important pass.

Dreadful were the feelings of the poor women on hearing this exposition of the case; for they easily understood that too capital an interest (the *summa rerum*) was now at stake to allow of any regard to minor interests, or what would be considered such in their present circumstances. The dreadful week already passed—their inauguration in misery—was yet fresh in their remembrance.The scars of suffering were impressed not only upon their memories, but upon their very persons and the persons of their children; and they knew that, where no speed had much chance of meeting the cravings of the chieftains, no test would be accepted, short of absolute exhaustion, that as much had been accomplished as could be accomplished. Weseloff, the Russian captive, has recorded the silent wretchedness with which the women and elder boys assisted in drawing the tent ropes. On the 5th of January all had been animation and the joyousness of indefinite expectation: now, on the contrary, a brief but bitter experience had taught them to take an amended calculation of what it was that lay before them.

One whole day and far into the succeeding night had the renewed flight continued: the sufferings had been greater than before; for the cold had been more intense, and many perished out of the living creatures through every class except only the camels, whose powers of endurance seemed equally adapted to cold and heat. The second morning, however, brought an alleviation to the distress. Snow had begun to fall; and, though not deep at present, it was easily foreseen that it soon would be so, and that, as a halt would in that case become unavoidable, no plan could be better than that of staying where they were, especially as the same cause would check the advance of the Cossacks. Here, then, was the last interval of comfort which gleamed upon the unhappy nation during their whole migration. For ten days the snow continued to fall with little intermission. At the end of that time keen, bright, frosty weather succeeded; the drifting had ceased. In three days the smooth expanse becamefirm enough to support the treading of the camels, and the flight was recommenced. But during the halt much domestic comfort had been enjoyed, and, for the last time, universal plenty. The cows and oxen had perished in such vast numbers on the previous marches, that an order was now issued to turn what remained to account by slaughtering the whole, and salting whatever part should be found to exceed the immediate consumption. This measure led to a scene of general banqueting, and even of festivity, amongst all who were not incapacitated for joyous emotions by distress of mind, by grief for the unhappy experience of the few last days, and by anxiety for the too gloomy future. Seventy thousand persons of all ages had already perished, exclusively of the many thousand allies who had been cut down by the Cossack sabre; and the losses in reversion were likely to be many more; for rumors began now to arrive from all quarters, by the mounted couriers whom the khan had despatched to the rear and to each flank as well as in advance, that large masses of the imperial troops were converging from all parts of Central Asia to the fords of the river Torgai, as the most convenient point for intercepting the flying tribes; and it was already well known that a powerful division was close in their rear, and was retarded only by the numerous artillery which had been judged necessary to support their operations. New motives were thus daily arising for quickening the motions of the wretched Kalmucks and for exhausting those who were previously but too much exhausted.

It was not until the 2d day of February that the khan's advanced guard came in sight of Ouchim, the defile amongthe hills of Moulgaldchares, in which they anticipated so bloody an opposition from the Cossacks. A pretty large body of these light cavalry had, in fact, preoccupied the pass by some hours; but the khan, having two great advantages,—namely, a strong body of infantry, who had been conveyed by sections of five on about two hundred camels, and some pieces of light artillery which he had not yet been forced to abandon,—soon began to make a serious impression upon this unsupported detachment, and they would probably at any rate have retired; but, at the very moment when they were making some dispositions in that view, Zebek-Dorchi appeared upon their rear with a body of trained riflemen who had distinguished themselves in the war with Turkey. These men had contrived to crawl unobserved over the cliffs which skirted the ravine, availing themselves of the dry beds of the summer torrents and other inequalities of the ground to conceal their movement. Disorder and trepidation ensued instantly in the Cossack files. The khan, who had been waiting with the *élite* of his heavy cavalry, charged furiously upon them. Total overthrow followed to the Cossacks, and a slaughter such as in some measure avenged the recent bloody extermination of their allies, the ancient *ouloss* of Feka-Zechorr. The slight horses of the Cossacks were unable to support the weight of heavy Polish dragoons and a body of trained *cameleers* (that is, cuirassiers mounted on camels). Hardy they were, but not strong, nor a match for their antagonists in weight; and their extraordinary efforts through the last few days to gain their present position had greatly diminished their powers for effecting an escape. Very few, in fact, *did* escape;and the bloody day of Ouchim became as memorable amongst the Cossacks as that which, about twenty days before, had signalized the complete annihilation of the Feka-Zechorr.

The road was now open to the river Igritch, and as yet even far beyond it to the Torgau; but how long this state of things would continue was every day more doubtful. Certain intelligence was now received that a large Russian army, well appointed in every arm, was advancing upon the Torgau under the command of General Traubenberg. This officer was to be joined on his route by ten thousand Bashkirs and pretty nearly the same amount of Kirghises,—both hereditary enemies of the Kalmucks,—both exasperated to a point of madness by the bloody trophies which Oubacha and Momotbacha had, in late years, won from such of their compatriots as served under the sultan. The czarina's yoke these wild nations bore with submissive patience, but not the hands by which it had been imposed; and accordingly, catching with eagerness at the present occasion offered to their vengeance, they sent an assurance to the czarina of their perfect obedience to her commands, and at the same time a message significantly declaring in what spirit they meant to execute them, namely, "that they would not trouble her Majesty with prisoners."

Here then arose, as before with the Cossacks, a race for the Kalmucks with the regular armies of Russia, and concurrently with nations as fierce and semi-humanized as themselves, besides that they were stung into threefold activity by the furies of mortified pride and military abasement under the eyes of the Turkish sultan. Theforces, and more especially the artillery, of Russia, were far too overwhelming to permit the thought of a regular opposition in pitched battles, even with a less dilapidated state of their resources than they could reasonably expect at the period of their arrival on the Torgau. In their speed lay their only hope,—in strength of foot, as before, and not in strength of arm. Onward, therefore, the Kalmucks pressed, marking the lines of their wide-extending march over the sad solitudes of the steppes by a never-ending chain of corpses. The old and the young, the sick man on his couch, the mother with her baby,—all were left behind. Sights such as these, with the many rueful aggravations incident to the helpless condition of infancy,—of disease and of female weakness abandoned to the wolves amidst a howling wilderness,—continued to track their course through a space of full two thousand miles; for so much at the least it was likely to prove, including the circuits to which they were often compelled by rivers or hostile tribes, from the point of starting on the Wolga until they could reach their destined halting-ground on the east bank of the Torgau. For the first seven weeks of this march their sufferings had been imbittered by the excessive severity of the cold; and every night—so long as wood was to be had for fires, either from the lading of the camels, or from the desperate sacrifice of their baggage-wagons, or (as occasionally happened) from the forests which skirted the banks of the many rivers which crossed their path—no spectacle was more frequent than that of a circle, composed of men, women, and children, gathered by hundreds round a central fire, all dead and stiff at the return of morninglight. Myriads were left behind from pure exhaustion, of whom none had a chance, under the combined evils which beset them, of surviving through the next twenty-four hours. Frost, however, and snow at length ceased to persecute; the vast extent of the march at length brought them into more genial latitudes; and the unusual duration of the march was gradually bringing them into the more genial seasons of the year. Two thousand miles had at least been traversed; February, March, April, were gone; the balmy month of May had opened; vernal sights and sounds came from every side to comfort the heart-weary travellers; and at last, in the latter end of May, they crossed the Torgau, and took up a position where they hoped to find liberty to repose themselves for many weeks in comfort as well as in security, and to draw such supplies from the fertile neighborhood as might restore their shattered forces to a condition for executing, with less of wreck and ruin, the large remainder of the journey.

Yes; it was true that two thousand miles of wandering had been completed, but in a period of nearly five months, and with the terrific sacrifice of at least two hundred and fifty thousand souls, to say nothing of herds and flocks past all reckoning. These had all perished,—ox, cow, horse, mule, ass, sheep, or goat; not one survived,—only the camels. These arid and adust creatures, looking like the mummies of some antediluvian animals, without the affections or sensibilities of flesh and blood,—these only still erected their speaking eyes to the eastern heavens, and had to all appearance come out from this long tempest of trial unscathed and unharmed. The khan, knowing how much he was individually answerable for the misery which had been sustained, must have wept tears even more bitter than those of Xerxes when he threw his eyes over the myriads whom he had assembled; for the tears of Xerxes were unmingled with compunction. Whatever amends were in his power he resolved to make by sacrifices to the general good of all personal regards; and accordingly, even at this point of their advance, he once more deliberately brought under review the whole question of the revolt. The question was formally debated before the council, whether, even at this point, they should untread their steps, and, throwing themselves upon the czarina's mercy, return to their old allegiance. In that case, Oubacha professed himself willing to become the scapegoat for the general transgression. This, he argued, was no fantastic scheme, but even easy of accomplishment; for the unlimited and sacred power of the khan, so well known to the empress, made it absolutely iniquitous to attribute any separate responsibility to the people. Upon the khan rested the guilt,—upon the khan would descend the imperial vengeance. This proposal was applauded for its generosity, but was energetically opposed by Zebek-Dorchi. Were they to lose the whole journey of two thousand miles? Was their misery to perish without fruit? True it was that they had yet reached only the half-way house; but, in that respect, the motives were evenly balanced for retreat or for advance. Either way they would have pretty nearly the same distance to traverse, but with this difference,—that, forwards, their route lay through lands comparatively fertile; backwards, through a blasted wilderness, rich only in memorial of their sorrow, and hideous to Kalmuck eyes by the trophies of their calamity. Besides, though the empress might accept an excuse for the past, would she the less forbear to suspect for the future? The czarina's *pardon* they might obtain; but could they ever hope to recover her *confidence?* Doubtless there would now be a standing presumption against them, an immortal ground of jealousy; and a jealous government would be but another name for a harsh one. Finally, whatever motives there ever had been for the revolt surely remained unimpaired by anything that had occurred. In reality, the revolt was, after all, no revolt, but (strictly speaking) a return to their old allegiance; since, not above one hundred and fifty years ago (namely, in the year 1616), their ancestors had revolted from the Emperor of China. They had now tried both governments; and for them China was the land of promise, and Russia the house of bondage.

Spite, however, of all that Zebek could say or do, the yearning of the people was strongly in behalf of the khan's proposal; the pardon of their prince, they persuaded themselves, would be readily conceded by the empress; and there is little doubt that they would at this time have thrown themselves gladly upon the imperial mercy; when suddenly all was defeated by the arrival of two envoys from Traubenberg. This general had reached the fortress of Orsk, after a very painful march, on the 12th of April; thence he set forwards towards Oriembourg, which he reached upon the 1st of June, having been joined on his route at various times through themonth of May by the Kirghises and a corps of ten thousand Bashkirs. From Oriembourg he sent forward his official offers to the khan, which were harsh and peremptory, holding out no specific stipulations as to pardon or impunity, and exacting unconditional submission as the preliminary price of any cessation from military operations. The personal character of Traubenberg, which was anything but energetic, and the condition of his army, disorganized in a great measure by the length and severity of the march, made it probable that, with a little time for negotiation, a more conciliatory tone would have been assumed. But, unhappily for all parties, sinister events occurred in the mean time, such as effectually put an end to every hope of the kind.

The two envoys sent forward by Traubenberg had reported to this officer that a distance of only ten days' march lay between his own head-quarters and those of the khan. Upon this fact transpiring, the Kirghises, by their prince Nourali, and the Bashkirs entreated the Russian general to advance without delay. Once having placed his cannon in position, so as to command the Kalmuck camp, the fate of the rebel khan and his people would be in his own hands, and they would themselves form his advanced guard. Traubenberg, however,—*why* has not been certainly explained,— refused to march, grounding his refusal upon the condition of his army and their absolute need of refreshment. Long and fierce was the altercation; but at length, seeing no chance of prevailing, and dreading above all other events the escape of their detested enemy, the ferocious Bashkirs went off in a body by forced marches. In six days they reachedthe Torgau, crossed by swimming their horses, and fell upon the Kalmucks, who were dispersed for many a league in search of food or provender for their camels. The first day's action was one vast succession of independent skirmishes, diffused over a field of thirty to forty miles in extent; one party often breaking up into three or four, and again (according to the accidents of ground) three or four blending into one; flight and pursuit, rescue and total overthrow, going on simultaneously, under all varieties of form, in all quarters of the plain. The Bashkirs had found themselves obliged, by the scattered state of the Kalmucks, to split up into innumerable sections; and thus, for some hours, it had been impossible for the most practised eye to collect the general tendency of the day's fortune. Both the khan and Zebek-Dorchi were at one moment made prisoners, and more than once in imminent danger of being cut down; but at length Zebek succeeded in rallying a strong column of infantry, which, with the support of the camel corps on each flank, compelled the Bashkirs to retreat. Clouds, however, of these wild cavalry continued to arrive through the next two days and nights, followed or accompanied by the Kirghises. These being viewed as the advanced parties of Traubenberg's army, the Kalmuck chieftains saw no hope of safety but in flight; and in this way it happened that a retreat, which had so recently been brought to a pause, was resumed at the very moment when the unhappy fugitives were anticipating a deep repose, without further molestation, the whole summer through.

It seemed as though every variety of wretchedness were predestined to the Kalmucks, and as if their sufferings were incomplete unless they were rounded and matured by all that the most dreadful agencies of summer's heat could superadd to those of frost and winter. To this sequel of their story we shall immediately revert, after first noticing a little romantic episode which occurred at this point between Oubacha and his unprincipled cousin Zebek-Dorchi.

There was, at the time of the Kalmuck flight from the Wolga, a Russian gentleman of some rank at the court of the khan, whom, for political reasons, it was thought necessary to carry along with them as a captive. For some weeks his confinement had been very strict, and in one or two instances cruel; but, as the increasing distance was continually diminishing the chances of escape, and perhaps, also, as the misery of the guards gradually withdrew their attention from all minor interests to their own personal sufferings, the vigilance of the custody grew more and more relaxed; until at length, upon a petition to the khan, Mr. Weseloff was formally restored to liberty; and it was understood that he might use his liberty in whatever way he chose, even for returning to Russia, if that should be his wish. Accordingly, he was making active preparations for his journey to St. Petersburg, when it occurred to Zebek-Dorchi that not improbably, in some of the battles which were then anticipated with Traubenberg, it might happen to them to lose some prisoner of rank, in which case the Russian Weseloff would be a pledge in their hands for negotiating an exchange. Upon this plea, to his own severe affliction, the

Russian was detained until the further pleasure of the khan. The khan's name, indeed, was used through the whole affair, but, as it seemed, with so little concurrence on his part, that, when Weseloff in a private audience humbly remonstrated upon the injustice done him and the cruelty of thus sporting with his feelings by setting him at liberty, and, as it were, tempting him into dreams of home and restored happiness only for the purpose of blighting them, the good-natured prince disclaimed all participation in the affair, and went so far in proving his sincerity as even to give him permission to effect his escape; and, as a ready means of commencing it without raising suspicion, the khan mentioned to Mr. Weseloff that he had just then received a message from the hetman of the Bashkirs, soliciting a private interview on the banks of the Torgau at a spot pointed out. That interview was arranged for the coming night; and Mr. Weseloff might go in the khan's *suite*, which on either side was not to exceed three persons. Weseloff was a prudent man, acquainted with the world, and he read treachery in the very outline of this scheme, as stated by the khan,— treachery against the khan's person. He mused a little, and then communicated so much of his suspicions to the khan as might put him on his guard; but, upon further consideration, he begged leave to decline the honor of accompanying the khan. The fact was, that three Kalmucks, who had strong motives for returning to their countrymen on the west bank of the Wolga, guessing the intentions of Weseloff, had offered to join him in his escape. These men the khan would probably find himself obliged to countenance in their project; so that it became a point of honor with Weseloff to conceal their intentions, and therefore to accomplish the evasion from the camp (of which the firststeps only would be hazardous), without risking the notice of the khan.

The district in which they were now encamped abounded through many hundred miles with wild horses of a docile and beautiful breed. Each of the four fugitives had caught from seven to ten of these spirited creatures in the course of the last few days. This raised no suspicion, for the rest of the Kalmucks had been making the same sort of provision against the coming toils of their remaining route to China. These horses were secured by halters, and hidden about dusk in the thickets which lined the margin of the river. To these thickets, about ten at night, the four fugitives repaired. They took a circuitous path which drew them as little as possible within danger of challenge from any of the outposts or of the patrols which had been established on the quarters where the Bashkirs lay, and in three quarters of an hour they reached the rendezvous. The moon had now risen; the horses were unfastened; and they were in the act of mounting, when the deep silence of the woods was disturbed by a violent uproar and the clashing of arms. Weseloff fancied that he heard the voice of the khan shouting for assistance. He remembered the communication made by that prince in the morning; and, requesting his companions to support him, he rode off in the direction of the sound. A very short distance brought him to an open glade in the wood, where he beheld four men contending with a party of at least nine or ten. Two of the four were dismounted at the very instant of Weseloff's arrival. One of these he recognized almost certainly as the khan, who was fighting hand to hand, but at great disadvantage, with two of the adverse horsemen. Seeing that no time was to be lost, Weseloff fired and brought down one of the two. His companions discharged their carabines at the same moment; and then all rushed simultaneously into the little open area. The thundering sound of about thirty horses, all rushing at once into a narrow space, gave the impression that a whole troop of cavalry was coming down upon the assailants, who accordingly wheeled about and fled with one impulse. Weseloff advanced to the dismounted cavalier, who, as he expected, proved to be the khan. The man whom Weseloff had shot was lying dead; and both were shocked, though Weseloff at least was not surprised, on stooping down and scrutinizing his features, to recognize a well-known confidential servant of Zebek-Dorchi. Nothing was said by either party. The khan rode off, escorted by Weseloff and his companions; and for some time a dead silence prevailed. The situation of Weseloff was delicate and critical. To leave the khan at this point was probably to cancel their recent services; for he might be again crossed on his path, and again attacked by the very party from whom he had just been delivered. Yet, on the other hand, to return to the camp was to endanger the chances of accomplishing the escape. The khan, also, was apparently revolving all this in his mind; for at length he broke silence and said, "I comprehend your situation; and, under other circumstances, I might feel it my duty to detain your companions; but it would ill become me to do so after the important service you have just rendered me. Let us turn a little to the left. There, where you see the watchfire, is an outpost. Attend me so far. I am then safe. You may turn and pursue your enterprise; for the circumstances under which you will appear as my escort are sufficient to shield you from all suspicion for the present. I regret having no better means at my disposal for testifying my gratitude. But, tell me, before we part, was it accident only which led you to my rescue? or had you acquired any knowledge of the plot by which I was decoyed into this snare?" Weseloff answered very candidly that mere accident had brought him to the spot at which he heard the uproar; but that, *having* heard it, and connecting it with the khan's communication of the morning, he had then designedly gone after the sound in a way which he certainly should not have done at so critical a moment unless in the expectation of finding the khan assaulted by assassins. A few minutes after they reached the outpost at which it became safe to leave the Tartar chieftain; and immediately the four fugitives commenced a flight which is, perhaps, without a parallel in the annals of travelling. Each of them led six or seven horses besides the one he rode; and by shifting from one to the other (like the ancient *desultors* of the Roman circus), so as never to burden the same horse for more than half an hour at a time, they continued to advance at the rate of two hundred miles in the twenty-four hours for three days consecutively. After that time, considering themselves beyond pursuit, they proceeded less rapidly, though still with a velocity which staggered the belief of Weseloff's friends in after years. He was, however, a man of high principle, and always adhered firmly to the details of his printed report. One of the circumstances there statedis, that they continued to pursue the route by which the Kalmucks had fled, never for an instant finding any difficulty in tracing it by the skeletons and other memorials of their calamities. In particular, he mentions vast heaps of money as part of the valuable property which it had been necessary to sacrifice. These heaps were found lying still untouched in the deserts. From these Weseloff and his companions took as much as they could conveniently carry; and this it was, with the price of their beautiful horses, which they afterwards sold at one of the Russian military settlements for about fifteen pounds apiece, which eventually enabled them to pursue their journey in Russia. This journey, as regarded Weseloff in particular, was closed by a tragical catastrophe. He was at that time young, and the only child of a doting mother. Her affliction under the violent abduction of her son had been excessive, and probably had undermined her constitution. Still she had supported it. Weseloff, giving way to the natural impulses of his filial affection, had imprudently posted through Russia to his mother's house without warning of his approach. He rushed precipitately into her presence; and she, who had stood the shocks of sorrow, was found unequal to the shock of joy too sudden and too acute. She died upon the spot.

We now revert to the final scenes of the Kalmuck flight. These it would be useless to pursue circumstantially through the whole two thousand miles of suffering which remained; for the character of that suffering was even more monotonous than on the former half of the flight, but also more severe. Its main elements were excessive heat, with the accompaniments of famine and thirst,but aggravated at every step by the murderous attacks of their cruel enemies, the Bashkirs and the Kirghises.

These people, "more fell than anguish, hunger, or the sea," stuck to the unhappy Kalmucks like a swarm of enraged hornets; and very often, whilst *they* were attacking them in the rear, their advanced parties and flanks were attacked with almost equal fury by the people of the country which they were traversing; and with good reason, since the law of self-preservation had now obliged the fugitive Tartars to plunder provisions and to forage wherever they passed. In this respect their condition was a constant oscillation of wretchedness; for sometimes, pressed by grinding famine, they took a circuit of perhaps a hundred miles, in order to strike into a land rich in the comforts of life. But in such a land they were sure to find a crowded population, of which every arm was raised in unrelenting hostility, with all the advantages of local knowledge, and with constant preoccupation of all the defensible positions, mountain passes, or bridges. Sometimes, again, wearied out with this mode of suffering, they took a circuit of perhaps a hundred miles, in order to strike into a land with few or no inhabitants; but in such a land they were sure to meet absolute starvation. Then, again, whether with or without this plague of starvation, whether with or without this plague of hostility in front, whatever might be the "fierce varieties" of their misery in this respect, no rest ever came to their unhappy rear; *post equitem sedet atra cura*; it was a torment like the undying worm of conscience; and, upon the whole, it presented a spectacle altogether unprecedented in the history of mankind. Private and personal malignity is not unfrequently immortal; but rare indeed is it to find the same pertinacity of malice in a nation. And what imbittered the interest was, that the malice was reciprocal. Thus far the parties met upon equal terms; but that equality only sharpened the sense of their dire inequality as to other circumstances. The Bashkirs were ready to fight "from morn to dewy eve." The Kalmucks, on the contrary, were always obliged to run: was it *from* their enemies as creatures whom they feared? No; but *towards* their friends,— towards that final haven of China,—as what was hourly implored by their wives and the tears of their children. But, though they fled unwillingly, too often they fled in vain,—being unwillingly recalled. There lay the torment. Every day the Bashkirs fell upon them; every day the same unprofitable battle was renewed. As a matter of course, the Kalmucks recalled part of their advanced guard to fight them. Every day the battle raged for hours, and uniformly with the same result; for, no sooner did the Bashkirs find themselves too heavily pressed, and that the Kalmuck march had been retarded by some hours, than they retired into the boundless deserts, where all pursuit was hopeless. But if the Kalmucks resolved to press forward, regardless of their enemies, in that case their attacks became so fierce and overwhelming that the general safety seemed likely to be brought into question; nor could any effectual remedy be applied to the case, even for each separate day, except by a most embarrassing halt and by countermarches that, to men in their circumstances, were almost worse than death. It will not be surprising that the irritation of such a systematic persecution, superaddedto a previous and hereditary hatred and accompanied by the stinging consciousness of utter impotence as regarded all effectual vengeance, should gradually have inflamed the Kalmuck animosity into the wildest expression of downright madness and frenzy. Indeed, long before the frontiers of China were approached, the hostility of both sides had assumed the appearance much more of a warfare amongst wild beasts than amongst creatures acknowledging the restraints of reason or the claims of a common nature. The spectacle became too atrocious; it was that of a host of lunatics pursued by a host of fiends.

On a fine morning in early autumn of the year 1771, Kien Long, the Emperor of China, was pursuing his amusements in a wild frontier district lying on the outside of the Great Wall. For many hundred square leagues the country was desolate of inhabitants, but rich in woods of ancient growth and overrun with game of every description. In a central spot of this solitary region the emperor had built a gorgeous hunting-lodge, to which he resorted annually for recreation and relief from the cares of government. Led onwards in pursuit of game, he had rambled to a distance of two hundred miles or more from this lodge, followed at a little distance by a sufficient military escort, and every night pitching his tent in a different situation, until at length he had arrived on the very margin of the vast central deserts of Asia. Here he was standing, by accident, at an opening of his pavilion, enjoying the morning sunshine, when suddenly to the westward there arose a vast, cloudy vapor, which by degrees expanded, mounted, and seemed to be slowlydiffusing itself over the whole face of the heavens. By and by this vast sheet of mist began to thicken towards the horizon and to roll forward in billowy volumes. The emperor's suite assembled from all quarters; the silver trumpets were sounded in the rear; and from all the glades and forest avenues began to trot forward towards the pavilion the yagers, half cavalry, half huntsmen, who composed the imperial escort. Conjecture was on the stretch to divine the cause of this phenomenon; and the interest continually increased in proportion as simple curiosity gradually deepened into the anxiety of uncertain danger. At first it had been imagined that some vast troops of deer or other wild animals of the chase had been disturbed in their forest haunts by the emperor's movements, or possibly by wild beasts prowling for prey, and might be fetching a compass by way of re-entering the forest grounds at some remoter points secure from molestation. But this conjecture was dissipated by the slow increase of the cloud and the steadiness of its motion. In the course of two hours the vast phenomenon had advanced to a point which was judged to be within five miles of the spectators; though all calculations of distance were difficult, and often fallacious, when applied to the endless expanses of the Tartar deserts. Through the next hour, during which the gentle morning breeze had a little freshened, the dusty vapor had developed itself far and wide into the appearance of huge aerial draperies, hanging in mighty volumes from the sky to the earth; and at particular points, where the eddies of the breeze acted upon the pendulous skirts of these aerial curtains, rents were perceived, sometimes taking the form of regular arches, portals, and windows, through which began dimly to gleam the heads of camels "indorsed" with human beings, and at intervals the moving of men and horses in tumultuous array, and then through other openings, or vistas, at far-distant points, the flashing of polished arms. But sometimes, as the wind slackened or died away, all those openings, of whatever form, in the cloudy pall, would slowly close, and for a time the whole pageant was shut up from view; although the growing din, the clamors, the shrieks and groans ascending from infuriated myriads, reported, in a language not to be misunderstood, what was going on behind the cloudy screen.

It was, in fact, the Kalmuck host, now in the last extremities of their exhaustion, and very fast approaching to that final stage of privation and intense misery beyond which few or none could have lived, but also, happily for themselves, fast approaching (in a literal sense) that final stage of their long pilgrimage at which they would meet hospitality on a scale of royal magnificence and full protection from their enemies. These enemies, however, as yet, still were hanging on their rear as fiercely as ever; though this day was destined to be the last of their hideous persecution. The khan had, in fact, sent forward couriers with all the requisite statements and petitions, addressed to the Emperor of China. These had been duly received, and preparations made in consequence to welcome the Kalmucks with the most paternal benevolence. But as these couriers had been despatched from the Torgau at the moment of arrival thither, and before the advance of Traubenberg had made it necessary for the khan to order a hasty renewal of the flight, the emperor had not lookedfor their arrival on their frontier until full three months after the present time. The khan had, indeed, expressly notified his intention to pass the summer heats on the banks of the Torgau, and to recommence his retreat about the beginning of September. The subsequent change of plan being unknown to Kien Long, left him for some time in doubt as to the true interpretation to be put upon this mighty apparition in the desert; but at length the savage clamors of hostile fury and the clangor of weapons unveiled to the emperor the true nature of those unexpected calamities which had so prematurely precipitated the Kalmuck measure.

Apprehending the real state of affairs, the emperor instantly perceived that the first act of his fatherly care for these erring children (as he esteemed them), now returning to their ancient obedience, must be, to deliver them from their pursuers. And this was less difficult than might have been supposed. Not many miles in the rear was a body of well-appointed cavalry, with a strong detachment of artillery, who always attended the emperor's motions. These were hastily summoned. Meantime it occurred to the train of courtiers that some danger might arise to the emperor's person from the proximity of a lawless enemy; and accordingly he was induced to retire a little to the rear. It soon appeared, however, to those who watched the vapory shroud in the desert, that its motion was not such as would argue the direction of the march to be exactly upon the pavilion, but rather in a diagonal line, making an angle of full forty-five degrees with that line in which the imperial *cortége* had been standing, and therefore with a distance continually increasing. Those who knew the country judged that the Kalmucks were making for a large fresh-water lake about seven or eight miles distant. They were right; and to that point the imperial cavalry was ordered up; and it was precisely in that spot, and about three hours after, and at noonday, on the 8th of September, that the great exodus of the Kalmuck Tartars was brought to a final close, and with a scene of such memorable and hellish fury as formed an appropriate winding up to an expedition in all its parts and details so awfully disastrous. The emperor was not personally present, or at least he saw whatever he *did* see from too great a distance to discriminate its individual features; but he records in his written memorial the report made to him of this scene by some of his own officers.

The Lake of Tengis, near the frightful Desert of Kobi, lay in a hollow amongst hills of a moderate height, ranging generally from two to three thousand feet high. About eleven o'clock in the forenoon the Chinese cavalry reached the summit of a road which led through a cradle-like dip in the mountains right down upon the margin of the lake. From this pass, elevated about two thousand feet above the level of the water, they continued to descend, by a very winding and difficult road, for an hour and a half; and during the whole of this descent they were compelled to be inactive spectators of the fiendish spectacle below. The Kalmucks, reduced by this time from about six hundred thousand souls to two hundred thousand, and after enduring for two months and a half the miseries we have previously described,—outrageous heat, famine, and the destroying cimeter ofthe Kirghises and the Bashkirs,—had for the last ten days been traversing a hideous desert, where no vestiges were seen of vegetation and no drop of water could be found. Camels and men were already so overladen that it was a mere impossibility that they should carry a tolerable sufficiency for the passage of this frightful wilderness. On the eighth day, the wretched daily allowance, which had been continually diminishing, failed entirely; and thus, for two days of insupportable fatigue, the horrors of thirst had been carried to the fiercest extremity. Upon this last morning, at the sight of the hills and the forest scenery, which announced to those who acted as guides the neighborhood of the Lake of Tengis, all the people rushed along with maddening eagerness to the anticipated solace. The day grew hotter and hotter, the people more and more exhausted; and gradually, in the general rush forwards to the lake, all discipline and command were lost,—all attempts to preserve a rearguard were neglected.

The wild Bashkirs rode in amongst the encumbered people and slaughtered them by wholesale, and almost without resistance. Screams and tumultuous shouts proclaimed the progress of the massacre; but none heeded,—none halted; all alike, pauper or noble, continued to rush on with maniacal haste to the waters,—all with faces blackened by the heat preying upon the liver, and with tongue drooping from the mouth. The cruel Bashkir was affected by the same misery, and manifested the same symptoms of his misery, as the wretched Kalmuck. The murderer was oftentimes in the same frantic misery as his murdered victim. Many, indeed (an ordinary effect of thirst), in both nations, had becomelunatic; and in this state, whilst mere multitude and condensation of bodies alone opposed any check to the destroying cimeter and the trampling hoof, the lake was reached; and to that the whole vast body of enemies rushed, and together continued to rush, forgetful of all things at that moment but of one almighty instinct. This absorption of the thoughts in one maddening appetite lasted for a single minute; but in the next arose the final scene of parting vengeance. Far and wide the waters of the solitary lake were instantly dyed red with blood and gore. Here rode a party of savage Bashkirs, hewing off heads as fast as the swaths fall before the mower's scythe; there stood unarmed Kalmucks in a death-grapple with their detested foes, both up to the middle in water, and oftentimes both sinking together below the surface, from weakness or from struggles, and perishing in each other's arms. Did the Bashkirs at any point collect into a cluster for the sake of giving impetus to the assault, thither were the camels driven in fiercely by those who rode them, generally women or boys; and even these quiet creatures were forced into a share in this carnival of murder by trampling down as many as they could strike prostrate with the lash of their forelegs. Every moment the water grew more polluted; and yet every moment fresh myriads came up to the lake and rushed in, not able to resist their frantic thirst, and swallowing large draughts of water visibly contaminated with the blood of their slaughtered compatriots. Wheresoever the lake was shallow enough to allow of men raising their heads above the water, there, for scores of acres, were to be seen all forms of ghastly fear, of agonizingstruggle, of spasm, of convulsion, of mortal conflict,—death, and the fear of death,—revenge, and the lunacy of revenge,—hatred, and the frenzy of hatred; until the neutral spectators, of whom there were not a few, now descending the eastern side of the lake, at length averted their eyes in horror. This horror, which seemed incapable of further addition, was, however, increased by an unexpected incident. The Bashkirs, beginning to perceive here and there the approach of the Chinese cavalry, felt it prudent—wheresoever they were sufficiently at leisure from the passions of the murderous scene—to gather into bodies. This was noticed by the governor of a small Chinese fort built upon an eminence above the lake; and immediately he threw in a broadside, which spread havoc amongst the

Bashkir tribe. As often as the Bashkirs collected into "*globes*" and "*turms*" as their only means of meeting the long line of descending Chinese cavalry, so often did the Chinese governor of the fort pour in his exterminating broadside; until at length the lake, at the lower end, became one vast seething caldron of human bloodshed and carnage. The Chinese cavalry had reached the foot of the hills; the Bashkirs, attentive to *their* movements, had formed; skirmishes had been fought; and, with a quick sense that the contest was henceforwards rapidly becoming hopeless, the Bashkirs and Kirghises began to retire. The pursuit was not as vigorous as the Kalmuck hatred would have desired; but, at the same time, the very gloomiest hatred could not but find, in their own dreadful experience of the Asiatic deserts, and in the certainty that these wretched Bashkirs had to repeat that same experience, asecond time, for thousands of miles, as the price exacted by a retributary Providence for their vindictive cruelty, not the very gloomiest of the Kalmucks or the least reflecting but found in all this a retaliatory chastisement more complete and absolute than any which their swords and lances could have obtained or human vengeance could have devised.

Here ends the tale of the Kalmuck wanderings in the desert; for any subsequent marches which awaited them were neither long nor painful. Every possible alleviation and refreshment for their exhausted bodies had been already provided by Kien Long with the most princely munificence; and lands of great fertility were immediately assigned to them in ample extent along the river Ily, not very far from the point at which they had first emerged from the wilderness of Kobi. But the beneficent attention of the Chinese emperor may be best stated in his own words, as translated into French by one of the Jesuit missionaries: "La nation des Torgotes (*savoir les Kalmuques*) arriva à Ily, toute *delabrée*, n'ayant ni de quoi vivre, ni de quoi se vêtir. Je l'avais prévu; et j'avais ordonné de faire en tout genre les provisions nécessaires pour pouvoir les secourir promptement; c'est ce qui a été exécuté. On a fait la division des terres; et on a assigné à chaque famille une portion suffisante pour pouvoir servir à son entretien, soit en la cultivant, soit en y nourrissant des bestiaux. On a donné à chaque particulier des étoffes pour l'habiller, des grains pour se nourrir pendant l'espace d'une année, des ustensiles pour le ménage et d'autres choses nécessaires: et outre celaplusieurs onces d'argent, pour se pourvoir de ce qu'on aurait pu oublier. On a designé des lieux particuliers, fertiles en pâturages; et on leur a donné des bœufs, moutons, etc., pour qu'ils pussent dans la suite travailler par eux-mêmes à leur entretien et à leur bienêtre."

These are the words of the emperor himself, speaking in his own person of his own paternal cares; but another Chinese, treating the same subject, records the munificence of this prince in terms which proclaim still more forcibly the disinterested generosity which prompted, and the delicate considerateness which conducted, this extensive bounty. He has been speaking of the Kalmucks, and he goes on thus: "Lorsqu'ils arrivèrent sur nos frontières (au nombre de plusieurs centaines de mille), quoique la fatigue extrême, la faim, la soif, et toutes les autres incommodités inséparables d'une très-longue et très pénible route en eussent fait périr presque autant, ils étaient réduits à la dernière misère; ils manquaient de tout. Il" (viz., l'empereur, Kien Long) "leur fit préparer des logemens conformes à leur manière de vivre; il leur fit distribuer des aliments et des habits; il leur fit donner des bœufs, des moutons, et des ustensiles, pour les mettre en état de former des troupeaux et de cultiver la terre, *et tout cela à ses propres frais*, qui se sont montés à des sommes immenses, sans compter l'argent qu'il a donné à chaque chef-de-famille, pour pourvoir à la subsistance de sa femme et de ses enfans."

Thus, after their memorable year of misery, the Kalmucks were replaced in territorial possessions, and in comfort equal, perhaps, or even superior, to that which they had enjoyed in Russia, and with superior politicaladvantages. But, if equal or superior, their condition was no longer the same; if not in degree, their social prosperity had altered in quality; for, instead of being a purely pastoral and vagrant people, they were now in circumstances which obliged them to become essentially dependent upon agriculture, and thus far raised in social rank, that, by the natural course of their habits and the necessities of life, they were effectually reclaimed from roving and from the savage customs connected with so unsettled a life. They gained also in political privileges, chiefly through the immunity from military service which their new relations enabled them to obtain. These were circumstances of advantage and gain. But one great disadvantage there was, amply to overbalance all other possible gain,—the chances were lost, or were removed to an incalculable distance, for their conversion to Christianity, without which in these times there is no absolute advance possible on the path of true civilization.

One word remains to be said upon the *personal* interests concerned in this great drama. The catastrophe in this respect was remarkable and complete. Oubacha, with all his goodness and incapacity of suspecting, had, since the mysterious affair on the banks of the Torgau, felt his mind alienated from his cousin. He revolted from the man that would have murdered him; and he had displayed his caution so visibly as to provoke a reaction in the bearing of Zebek-Dorchi and a displeasure which all his dissimulation could not hide. This had produced a feud, which, by keeping them aloof, had probably saved the life of Oubacha; for the friendship of Zebek-Dorchi was more fatal than his open enmity.After the settlement on the Ily this feud continued to advance, until it came under the notice of the emperor on occasion of a visit which all the Tartar chieftains made to his majesty at his hunting-lodge in 1772. The emperor informed himself accurately of all the particulars connected with the transaction, of all the rights and claims put forward, and of the way in which they would severally affect the interests of the Kalmuck people. The consequence was, that he adopted the cause of Oubacha, and repressed the pretensions of Zebek-Dorchi, who, on his part, so deeply resented this discountenance to his ambitious projects, that, in conjunction with other chiefs, he had the presumption even to weave nets of treason against the emperor himself. Plots were laid, were detected, were baffled; counterplots were constructed upon the same basis, and with the benefit of the opportunities thus offered.

Finally Zebek-Dorchi was invited to the imperial lodge, together with all his accomplices; and, under the skilful management of the Chinese nobles in the emperor's establishment, the murderous artifices of these Tartar chieftains were made to recoil upon themselves; and the whole of them perished by assassination at a great imperial banquet; for the Chinese morality is exactly of that kind which approves in everything the *lex talionis*:—

"....lex nec justior ulla est (as *they* think)

Quam necis artifices arte perire sua."

So perished Zebek-Dorchi, the author and originator of the great Tartar *exodus*. Oubacha, meantime, and his people were gradually recovering from the effects of theirmisery and repairing their losses. Peace and prosperity, under the gentle rule of a fatherly lord paramount, redawned upon the tribes; their household *lares*, after so harsh a translation to distant climates, found again a happy reinstatement in what had, in fact, been their primitive abodes; they found themselves settled in quiet sylvan scenes, rich in all the luxuries of life, and endowed with the perfect loveliness of Arcadian beauty. But from the hills of this favored land, and even from the level grounds, as they approach its western border, they still look out upon that fearful wilderness which once beheld a nation in agony,—the utter extirpation of nearly half a million from amongst its numbers, and for the remainder a storm of misery so fierce that in the end (as happened also at Athens during the Peloponnesian war from a different form of misery) very many lost their memory; all records of their past life were wiped out as with a sponge,—utterly erased and cancelled; and many others lost their reason, some in a gentle form of pensive melancholy, some in a more restless form of feverish delirium and nervous agitation, and others in the fixed forms of tempestuous mania, raving frenzy, or moping idiocy. Two great commemorative monuments arose in after years to mark the depth and permanence of the awe, the sacred and reverential grief, with which all persons looked back upon the dread calamities attached to the year of the tiger,—all who had either personally shared in those calamities and had themselves drunk from that cup of sorrow, or who had effectually been made witnesses to their results and associated with their relief. Two great monuments, we say; first of all, one in the religious solemnity, enjoined by the Dalai lama, called in the Tartar language a *Romanang*, that is, a national commemoration, with music the most rich and solemn, of all the souls who departed to the rest of paradise from the afflictions of the desert. This took place about six years after the arrival in China. Secondly, another, more durable, and more commensurate to the scale of the calamity and to the grandeur of this national exodus, in the mighty columns of granite and brass erected by the emperor, Kien Long, near the banks of the Ily. These columns stand upon the very margin of the *steppes*, and they bear a short but emphatic inscription to the following effect:—

By the will of God,
Here, upon the brink of these deserts,
Which from this point begin and stretch away,
Pathless, treeless, waterless,
For thousands of miles, and along the margins of many mighty nations,
Rested from their labors and from great afflictions,
Under the shadow of the Chinese Wall,
And by the favor of KIEN LONG, God's Lieutenant upon Earth,
The ancient Children of the Wilderness,—the Torgote Tartars,—
Flying before the wrath of the Grecian czar;
Wandering sheep who had strayed away from the Celestial Empire in the
year 1616,
But are now mercifully gathered again, after infinite sorrow,
Into the fold of their forgiving shepherd.
Hallowed be the spot forever,
and
Hallowed be the day—September 8, 1771!
Amen.

FOOTNOTE:

[A] Tailgean, or the Holy Offspring, a name supposed to have been applied by the Druids to St. Patrick, previous to his arrival in Ireland.—*O'Brien's Irish Dictionary.*

Milton Keynes UK
Ingram Content Group UK Ltd.
UKHW030625061024
449204UK00004B/308